Second Chance

LIVING WITH A
RESCUED DOG

D1280279

Judy & Larry Elsden

RINGPRESS

RINGPRESS

Published by INTERPET PUBLISHING
Vincent Lane, Dorking, Surrey, RH4 3YX
United Kingdom

First published 1994. This edition published 2002.
© 1994 Ringpress Books Limited & Judy & Larry Elsden
All rights reserved

ISBN 1 86054 079 1

Printed by Kyodo Printing Company Pty, Singapore

Contents

Dedication

To man's best friend – the dog – and to those special people who go to his aid when others have failed him.

Acknowledgements

Writing this book has only been possible because of the support and assistance we have been given by a large number of welfare organisations and by concerned individuals.

From the beginning of this project, we have received enormous cooperation from the staff, at all levels, of the Wood Green Animal Shelters. No question or request has been too difficult, and we are very grateful for all the help that has been given, and for their permission to use many of the photographs included.

We are grateful to the following for their help and kindness:
Battersea Dogs Home, and David Cavill at Bellmead who took time out of a busy schedule to answer our questions.

Dogs for the Disabled and Hearing Dogs for the Deaf for providing case histories and permission to use their photographs.
Numerous breed and general rescue organisations, particularly Yorkshire Terrier Rescue, Rottweiler Welfare, and Leah and Harry Lovett.

We are grateful to Jilly Cooper who took time to talk about her dogs and gave permission for us to publish the photograph of herself with her dogs. Our thanks also to Loyd Grossman who gave us permission to publish the story of his dog Bally, and to reproduce a photograph of himself with Bally.

Finally, we owe a great debt to all those wonderful people who have given homes to rescued dogs. They took us into their homes, showed us their dogs, told us stories of their successes and sometimes their failures, found us photographs, and made us welcome. Without their help and inspiration, this book could not have been written.

Foreword

Animal welfare in general, and dogs' homes in particular, have fulfilled a need in society for over a hundred years. The support given to this need by the public comes in many ways, and, of course, the reason for their existence is a reflection and censure upon those elements of society who allow the birth of far more puppies than suitable homes can be provided for.

This is not to say that all those who allow this to happen are irresponsible, but the fact is that there is a large surplus of animals coming into the care of animal welfare organisations for whatever reasons. Much of the funding needed to care for those animals brought into care comes through donations, or from the people kind enough to provide a new home for those unwanted pets. Many of these animals are pure-bred, so it is simply not true that it is only the cross-bred or mongrel which is abandoned or unwanted

Judy and Larry Elsden's book indicates the importance to humans and canines of the role played by animal welfare organisations and shelters, including the breed rescue groups. Most importantly, it identifies, under appropriate chapter headings, the considerations to be made when choosing one of these special companions.

Second Chance – Living with a Rescued Dog is a very important reference work for those who already have dogs within the household, for those who are considering taking a dog into the family home, and for organisations and breeders who seek to address the welfare of man's best friend.

I recommend the reading of this book to anyone who has a regard for our canine friends.

Graham Fuller
Wood Green Animal Shelters.

Sam: Rehomed from Wood Green Animal Shelters.

Preface

When we started this book, the intention was to produce a useful guide to the owner or prospective owner of a rescued dog. As we gathered material together, we realised that the whole subject of rescued dogs, the organisations working for them, and the people who give them homes, is a major story in its own right. Part of this book sets out to tell some small portion of this story.

Writing this book has been a mixture of pleasure and sorrow. Pleasure at all the happy dogs and wonderful owners that we have met and talked to; sorrow at the long list of cases of neglect and cruelty that we have found. However, if by writing this book we can help some of those who have done such wonderful work in providing happy and loving homes for rescued dogs, and if we can persuade others to join them, then the book will have been worthwhile.

Judy and Larry Elsden.

Chapter One

THE DOGS IN NEED
OF RESCUE

WHAT IS A RESCUED DOG?

For many of us, the companionship of a dog is one of life's great pleasures. It is companionship rather than ownership: for many of us would debate whether we own the dog, or whether the dog owns us. If the chosen dog is a rescued dog, then you have the additional satisfaction of knowing that you have given the dog a second chance in life after the inability of the previous owner, for whatever cause, to provide a home.

This book is about the ownership of a particular type of dog. The type is to be found in all breeds (some breeds to a greater extent than others), in crossbreeds and mongrels, large dogs and small dogs, pretty little cuddly dogs and big, ugly dogs that only an enthusiast would call attractive. The type has one characteristic which is common to all of them: the dog is either unwanted, or at least unloved by his nominal owner, or more tragically, his owner can no longer look after him. All too frequently such dogs need to be found a new home. These dogs are usually known as "rescued dogs" – a description that has nothing to do with those breeds which serve mankind by finding lost children, or with the legendary St Bernard, complete with its barrel of brandy attached to its collar.

In this book we have set out to look at the pleasures of giving a happy future to a rescued dog, and the reward of knowing that you have saved a dog from either destruction or a miserable life. We will look at the problems you may encounter and, hopefully, provide some answers, with the aim of helping you to achieve a successful relationship with your dog.

THE SAVIOURS

Those who provide a new home for an unwanted dog, and those who work to rescue and re-home such dogs can justly be described as saints. There can be no doubt that those most deserving of canonisation are the workers in the numerous dog welfare organisations, frequently not only unpaid but often spending their own money for the cause. They are the ones who live close to the heartbreaks of the dogs who are either unwanted or ill-used by the community in which they live. The rescue workers can tell many tragic stories, ranging from the dog who, having spent many years as a much-loved family pet, finds himself homeless on the death of his owner, to the dog, ill-treated – mentally or physically or both – who has to be rescued from a cruel or neglectful home.

While the rescue workers are at the sharp end of what is a constant battle, those who offer a home to such a dog require qualities which go beyond a willingness to merely provide food and shelter. A dog who changes homes, for whatever reason, is likely to have problems which would not occur in one who has lived as a loved member of a family from puppyhood. A child from a broken home is more likely to have problems with society than the one from a stable home. The same problems of adjustment are equally likely for the dog whose background is not one of tender loving care, or one who has lost, through no fault of his own, the security of a caring owner. As the owner of a rescued dog you may require a vast amount of patience, sympathy and understanding in order to help your dog build a new life with you.

THE DOG'S MIND

The love affair between man and dog goes back to the time when both shared a cave. This relationship was founded on man and dog working together for their own mutual good and protection, and developed to shared love and companionship between owner and pet. Today there are still dogs who work in many ways for the good of man. However, at this stage we are focusing on the dog as a friend and companion, living as part of a normal household. It is immaterial whether the dog is pure-bred or mongrel, rescued or bought from a breeder.

To us, a house without a dog is not a home. Both of us have lived with dogs all our lives and cannot conceive life without at least one four-legged character sharing almost every aspect of it. The first dog that could be considered as coming within the rescued category was a tiny, skinny, brown puppy, probably about three to four months of age, whom we named Micky. We found him when we were living in Germany. He was sitting on a farmyard manure heap, attempting to eat the rather decayed head of a duck. What happened to his mother or the rest of the litter we never knew. For two cigarettes, he became ours. In his short life, Micky had already acquired the ability to cope with the problems of life. He was good-natured, intelligent and confident, and he quickly decided that life with us was far preferable to trying to scrounge an existence around the farmyard. In return, he gave us his total loyalty and love. He developed into a small, smooth-coated dog with big brown eyes and a gentle nature. He showed no signs of any particular breed and could only be described as a mongrel. However, we loved him, and for two years he was an important part of the family. Although he had no financial value, to us he was priceless – so much so that when we had to return to England we brought him with us through quarantine.

At the first opportunity we visited him in his 'prison'. While he was overjoyed to see us, he was obviously pining. Unfortunately, there was no alternative other than to visit him as often as possible, in the hope that he would realise that we still existed and loved him. However, after four months we had a letter from the vet at the kennel informing us that Micky had died from hardpad – a disease which took the lives of so many dogs in those days. Although it is over forty years ago that he died, we still remember him, along with so many other dogs that have given us their love.

Micky's story illustrates one of the most attractive aspects of the dog. Once a dog has given you his love and trust, it is almost impossible, as far as the dog is concerned, to break that relationship. No amount of indifference or neglect will destroy the feeling that the dog has for its owner. A dog will greet you after an absence with the same enthusiasm, whether it is the first time you have left it in its life, or whether it is the umpteenth time in a long life together. Your cross words or bad temper may cause a temporary droop of its tail or dropping of its ears, but it will seize the first opportunity to come back and comfort you and try to restore your relationship. We can think of no other living creature who gives so much and asks for so little.

ESTABLISHING A RELATIONSHIP

Dog psychologists frequently attempt to reduce the relationship between a dog and his owner to a formula which, if applied, can solve all the questions of how to achieve a successful life together. While much of this can be useful to someone setting out for the first time to own a dog, such an approach, if used without thought, can be as harmful and stultifying as attempting to apply a similar approach to a human relationship. One such formula is a list of things that you should not allow your dog to do.

This includes, for example, when the owner returns after an absence from his dog and is greeted by jumps of joy and the demand to be made a fuss of, that the dog should be ignored and taught that love and affection are given at the owner's discretion and are not available on demand. The list also states that any attempt your dog makes to attract your attention with a bark or scratching paw in the hope of a walk or a biscuit, should be similarly ignored, and that the dog shouldalways be fed after his human family and always fed inferior food. The theory behind all this is to establish the owner as the dominant partner. While agreeing that any human being should be capable of dominating a dog – after all, the human holds almost all the cards – we prefer to aim for a relationship based on mutual respect and affection.

It has been suggested that a dog is incapable of love for his owner, and that his attitude is based on subservient self-preservation in order to obtain food and protection. Our dogs are always delighted to see us after we have been away from them, they are unhappy when we are not with them, they are anxious to please us, keen to comfort us when we are miserable, laugh with us when we are happy, and protect us when they think there is danger. To us, this is love to a degree which many human couples would envy.

Dogs are trained to serve man in numerous ways. Some of these tasks use abilities in the dog, such as sense of smell, that man does not have or which are not developed to the same extent. Other tasks such as the guide dog for the blind, use the dog's senses to replace those which the human has lost. While all these tasks in the service of mankind are of immense value and must never be forgotten, the vast majority of dogs serve mankind simply as companions and friends. What greater service can we ask than for the dog to be there when we need him. If you have never owned a dog before, then try it and see the pleasures that one can bring you.

A dog will possibly decide that one person in the household – probably the one who feeds him, and with whom he spends most of his time – is his very special friend. However, the dog will very likely bond to the entire household as if it was a single entity. If one member of the household is away, then the dog's eyes will be on the front door and his ears alert to the sound of that person's return. The dog will be restless and alert until the household is complete again. Then, after greeting the absentee, the dog will relax, content that all is, once again, alright with his world.

REASONS FOR RESCUE
The success of your relationship with your rescued dog depends, to a considerable extent, on the dog's background and the reasons why he became a rescued dog. Knowledge of the dog's background can be of considerable help in deciding why he behaves as he does, and what action you need to take, if any, to help him fit into his new life with you.

There are probably five identifiable reasons why a dog becomes in need of rescue:

1. Loss of owner.
2. The dog is unsuitable for the owner, or the owner is unsuitable for the dog.
3. The stray dog – the dog never having had an owner, in the full sense of the term.
4. The dog is untrained or has been misused.
5. The rogue dog.

In addition, considerations of size, coat, breed, etc. can affect the issue, and these may even be contributory factors to the dog's need of being rescued.

LOSS OF OWNER
The most tragic and, in many cases, the easiest category to take into your home is the dog who, having lived for much of his life with a loving, caring owner, loses his owner through no fault of his own. Many such dogs spend much of their lives living in a family. First one partner dies, and the dog and the survivor

continue their lives together. Often the dog plays a major part as sole companion and comforter to the widow or widower, until he or she also dies.

Alternatively the owner may have to give up their dog as a result of some change in the owner's circumstances. The dog who has been loved, well-trained and cared for, is suddenly homeless, unwanted, and without the owner to whom he has given his trust and friendship. The dog has committed no sin and is perfectly well-behaved – his world has suddenly fallen apart, for reasons which he does not understand.

At first the dog may be suspicious and unresponsive to his new owner, but eventually, although we believe that he will not forget his former home, he will come to accept that you too love and care for him, and that, with you, he has found sanctuary. Giving a new life to such a dog can be extremely rewarding.

UNSUITABILITY

Many dogs have to be rehomed because the original owner made the wrong decision in their choice of dog. The person who is attracted by the beautiful dog advertising emulsion paint may have no concept of the amount of daily work involved in grooming and bathing such a dog. The dog may be well treated in every other way, but if the long coat becomes an insanitary mess, it could eventually become so bad that it is a health hazard to both dog and owner. Then the owner feels he cannot cope, and disposes of the dog. The answer is to have the coat clipped short and kept that way, but then the dog no longer looks like the one in the advertisement. As its new owner, you will have to decide whether you have the time and the enthusiasm to keep the full-coated dog groomed and bathed, or whether you have it clipped short. We know many owners of heavy-coated breeds who claim that they find an hour or more of grooming and brushing each day to be extremely therapeutic.

The difficulty of keeping a heavy-coated dog groomed and clean is only one example of why a dog may have to be rehomed because he was unsuitable for his owner's life style. Many people do not grasp that today's adorable, tiny puppy can be tomorrow's 100lb adult, who is quite unsuitable to be kept in a small upstairs flat. It is also not unusual for a husband to decide that he would like a large, macho breed, forgetting that he is at work all day and that the job of training, exercising and controlling the dog will be far beyond the capabilities of his petite wife. The 'Christmas Present Dog', bought on a whim as a present, and then unwanted by the family when the novelty has worn off, also falls into this category.

To the new owner, the dog that is rehomed because his previous owner bought the wrong dog, or, in some cases, should not have bought a dog at all, presents the least number of problems with regard to rehoming. In the majority of such cases, there is nothing wrong with the dog that your love and understanding will not cure, and the dog will welcome someone who cares for his needs.

NO REAL OWNER

The third category is the dog who has never really had an owner. This group includes both stray dogs, and the dog who, although legally owned, has been totally ignored by his nominal owner. Many people own a dog without taking the slightest interest in him, although they may go as far as feeding him when he comes home after a day roaming the streets. Such dogs will have become street-wise, intelligent and self-sufficient in order to survive. We have all seen the dog that trots up one side of a busy street until he reaches traffic lights or a pedestrian crossing. He will wait until the traffic stops, cross the road, and go back the way he came on the other side of the street. Such dogs have found out how to exist without the aid of man, and they probably only acknowledge humans as being something to be feared.

An example of this type is a medium-sized mongrel bitch, named Bambi. She was found living in an abandoned car, having made the back seat into a cozy nest. When found she was probably about four years old, and how long she had lived there nobody knows. She had no objection to being caught, although she was wary of men. Five attempts to find her a home failed. She just walked, or in many cases, jumped out. Finally, as a last hope, one of the staff at the animal shelter took her home. While still remaining a very odd little dog, she has settled there and has been part of the household for eleven years. She still retains many of the attributes of the undomesticated dog that she once was, and her owner has had to accept that Bambi will occasionally decide to sleep on top of the wardrobe, or hide in some odd spot. An awful lot of patience and love has gone into giving Bambi the confidence in her mistress that has persuaded her that being safe, warm and fed in a home is preferable to fending for herself from the back of an old car.

THE ILL-TREATED

The group of rescued dogs that cause the greatest amount of distress to those who have to deal with them are those who have been callously neglected or, even worse, those who have been subjected to deliberate cruelty. It is not unusual for a dog to be left behind – shut in the house or a shed – when their owner moves home, having decided that they no longer want him. Unless a neighbour investigates, the dog starves to death. In one case, the dog's owner moved out of a rented furnished flat, taking the furniture but leaving the dog behind. Dogs are frequently left tied to gate posts, if they are lucky, close to someone who will do something about it. But on other occasions the dog is left in an isolated place where the chances of being found before it is too late are remote. A modern alternative is to push the dog out of a car on a busy motorway. Whether people who do this are attracted by the opportunity for a fast getaway, or whether they hope that the dog will be quickly run over, we can only speculate.

When you bear in mind that the whole country is covered with organisations

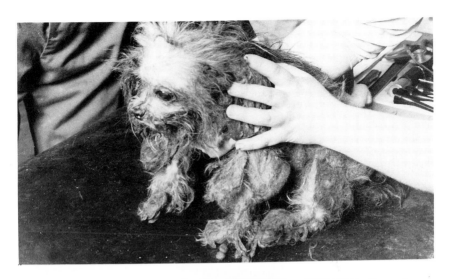

BEFORE: One of forty dogs removed from a house by the RSPCA. Tragically, twenty-seven of them were beyond help and had to be destroyed.

AFTER: Staff at Wood Green Animal Shelters nursed the remaining dogs back to health. This little dog, clean, fit, and healthy, is now in a loving home.
Wood Green Animal Shelters.

who will help people who cannot or will not keep their dogs, it is impossible to understand the lengths that some owners will go to in order to get rid of dogs by neglectful or cruel means. Sometimes the fault is in being misguided rather than cruel. Among our case histories is a large dog called Duke. At the age of six months, he had a front leg amputated after a car accident. His owner loved him and kept him. The owner then lost his job, but he still kept Duke. He sold his car to help pay for food for the dog and himself, but then he lost his home. Deciding that he could no longer keep Duke – and that no one would give a home to a three-legged dog – the owner walked Duke ten miles to a vet, with the intention of having him put down. When they got there, Duke was in a state of collapse with his one front paw bleeding badly. The vet refused to put him down, and contacted a breed welfare organisation. After two months of care, Duke was rehomed and now lives happily with four other dogs.

Deliberate cruelty cases are found all too frequently in a country that claims to be a nation of dog lovers. Dogs are stabbed with garden forks, tied up in barbed wire, thrown in rivers with bricks tied to their collar, used to stub out cigarettes, and – a fairly recent revival of an ancient cruelty – used for dog fighting. The list of ingenious barbarities practised by man on the dog is endless and horrifying. Dogs who have been treated in this way owe nothing to mankind, and they can be excused if they hate and fear all human beings.

In general, the dog's most likely reaction is total suspicion and dislike, coupled with a determination, if the dog is big enough and tough enough, to attack before he is attacked. Alternatively, the dog may have been beaten into a servile submission, when they are grateful if they are not ill-treated, and will show a grovelling anxiety to please. Sadly, a very small percentage of those who have decided that attack is the best policy have developed an aggressive attitude to humans that cannot be reversed. While it is possible to rehome such dogs, there are few owners expert and courageous enough to cope with them, and an attempt to do so by an inexperienced handler is likely to fail and may end in tragedy. Fortunately, the majority of ill-treated dogs are capable of being rehabilitated by love, care and a lot of patience. Their confidence can be rebuilt, and they will respond by giving their new owner their trust and affection. Anyone giving a home to such a dog must always be aware of what happened to him in the past. A sudden shout, or a raised arm – even if it is not aimed at the dog – may trigger unpleasant memories and undo weeks of work.

ROGUE DOGS
The final category of dogs looking for a new home is one which, in our opinion, should never be considered for rehoming. Many people will argue that no dog is basically bad and that any behavioural faults he may show are faults of his upbringing by man. This is true of the vast majority. There is, however, a very small percentage that can only be described as "rogue dogs" who are incapable of fitting into the community. This may be the result of man failing

to appreciate the results of mating two dogs whose combined temperaments produce an unstable animal, or it may be what, in a human, would be considered mental illness. Whatever the cause, any attempt to fit such dogs into the modern world is likely to result in disaster. Furthermore, it can be argued that the adverse publicity generated by incidents involving such dogs damages the image of dogs in general, causes restrictions to be placed on all dogs, and results in the mass of well-behaved dogs suffering because of the behaviour of a minute minority.

The true reason why your dog became in need of a new home may not be apparent from the information given by the previous owner. Many such owners are unwilling to admit that their own attitude or mistake has been the cause of them wishing to dispose of the dog.

CHOOSING A RESCUED DOG

SIZE
If you are contemplating taking on a rescued dog, then there are other factors which you may take into account before making your choice. The first one of these is size – large or small, or somewhere in between. A large dog often appeals to the man in the household. He likes a dog that he can pat without bending down. He is also wants to take a dog for his daily walk without risking damage to his masculine image, which he fears would be the case with a small and pretty little toy dog. Many women also like a large dog for the security that he can give them, and they are very successful as owners. There is nothing wrong in hoping that your family pet will also be the family guard, and in this case the large dog has obvious advantages. The tiny dog will still do his best to defend you, but may suffer as a result. Your relationship with a large dog can be a very satisfying one of mutual respect.

A little dog has one major advantage – apart from the obvious plus points of ease of control, and the small amount of space that they take up – it is much easier for the two of you to be together almost all of the time. There are no problems if you want your dog to share your armchair, or go sightseeing tucked under your arm. Friends may not welcome a large, hairy monster into their home, but they will have no objections to the small dog that sits on your lap. The more time that you and your dog spend together, the closer the relationship, and "smallness" makes this easier. Your own living accommodation and its location must also be taken into account in deciding the size of dog that you wish to own. An upstairs flat may be fine for a small dog but totally unsuitable for a large dog, although, to a certain extent, the amount of effort you are prepared to put into looking after your dog can modify this aspect. We have known large dogs kept successfully in urban conditions up three flights of stairs, but only by dedicated owners who work very hard for their dogs.

PURE-BRED OR MONGREL

You will have to decide between a mongrel (which, incidentally, should not be considered as a term of disparagement) and a pure-bred dog of a particular breed. This is largely a matter of personal preference – they are all dogs, with the same advantages and disadvantages of the species. It is possible that the mongrel has a slight edge in physical fitness and longevity, which is often described as hybrid vigour, although it can be argued that this is only because of the survival of the fittest. Pure-bred puppies that are carefully reared and protected have a high survival rate, while mongrel puppies are often left to fend for themselves to a considerable degree. Those that survive have got to be tough.

Pure-bred dogs owe their existence to the needs of mankind. We required dogs to carry out a multitude of tasks ranging from hunting to ladies' lap dogs. Having developed a dog for a particular job, man set out to perpetuate these qualities by selective and controlled breeding. Although many of the functions for which these breeds were produced no longer exist, man has maintained them in their developed form, and almost all breeds have their supporters who enjoy a particular breed both for its appearance and for its character. One of the attractions of a pure-bred dog is that a prospective owner knows that its size, colour, general appearance, and character are reasonably predictable.

If you decide that there is particular breed you want, then it is highly likely that there is a breed rescue society who will advise you and help you obtain one. The availability of pure-bred dogs who require rescue is in proportion to the overall popularity of the breed. The more the general public think that they would like to own a particular breed, the more members of that breed will come into the categories listed in the early part of this chapter. You should not look on acquiring a pure-bred rescued dog as a cheap way of obtaining a pedigree dog of a breed that would otherwise have cost you several hundred pounds. Welfare organizations will, quite rightly, usually take steps to prevent to you from turning your rescue dog to financial advantage. Bitches will probably be neutered, pedigrees and Kennel Club registration documents will be withheld, and the legal ownership of the dog will be retained by the rescue organisation. If you want to breed, exhibit at dog shows, or boast about the number of Champions in its pedigree, then you must pay the going price for such a dog. If you have no strong preference for a particular breed of dog, then you may decide to choose a mongrel. By the time the dog arrives in the rescue system he will probably be fully grown, and you will be able to see what his final size and appearance is going to be. You will also be able to make a reasonable assessment of his temperament. He will probably be a "character" with a mind of his own and a sense of humour. You will have a lot of fun with him, almost certainly a few problems, but, above all, you will have the satisfaction of knowing that you have helped a dog from the group that is always the one in most need of help.

ABOVE: A dog may need to be rehomed because the owner is failing to cope with it, either due to its size or to its behavioural problems.

LEFT: All too often dogs are abandoned because the owner is not prepared to take on the responsibility of caring for an animal. This six-week-old cross-bred puppy was dumped in a cardboard box outside Battersea Dogs' Home on Boxing Day.

ABOVE: Greyhounds are often in need of rehoming after their racing careers have come to an end and they make delightful companions. Penny, a Greyhound bitch, was sent to Wood Green Animal Shelters to be destroyed after allegedly attacking children. She was saved at the last moment by a visiting journalist, who describes her as "the most elegant, affectionate, faithful, well-behaved animal I have ever met."
Wood Green Animal Shelters.

LEFT: Cross-breeds and mongrels make up the majority of the population at all-breed rescue homes. They are often great characters with their own sense of humour. Sooty was adopted from Wood Green Animal Shelters when he was fourteen weeks of age. According to his owners he "put his paws through the bars and cried to be taken home. He is a real scruff – bouncy, exuberant, brainless – but beautiful!"
G.W. Farmer.

Pure-bred dogs make up a sizeable proportion of the dogs who need rehoming.

Trixie, the Saluki, rehomed herself. She turned up at a riding stable, caked with mud, and had probably been living rough for several weeks. Her present owner spent weeks trying to trace an owner, without success. She was then found to be in whelp; she produced three puppies who were all found homes. Seven years later she is living happily with her rescuers, and is firm friends with canine companion, Mandy.

Wood Green Animal Shelters.

The popularity of television programmes such as 'One Man And His Dog' meant that demand for Border Collies as pets soared. But this intelligent, active breed does not always settle well in the domestic environment, and all too often the "uncontrollable" pet ends up in a Rescue centre.

Luca, the cross-breed, needed rehoming when his previous owners discovered that their child was allergic to dogs. Luca's new owner said: "I took one look at those ears and I was smitten!"

Wood Green Animal Shelters.

CHOOSING YOUR RESCUED DOG

LEFT: If you have children it is essential to select a dog who has a tolerant, gentle nature, and will enjoy all the extra attention!

ABOVE: Many dogs need rehoming because the owners failed to appreciate how big the dog would grow and how expensive it would be to feed. Make sure you take this into consideration before selecting a giant breed.

RIGHT: Rottweilers have been the subject of bad publicity, and the breed as a whole has suffered from it. However, you should not think about taking on a big, guarding breed unless you have the experience to cope with any training difficulties that may arise.

ABOVE: A little dog has lots of personality, and is a better choice if you have limited space.

Carol Ann Johnson.

LEFT: A long-coated dog requires regular grooming, and you must make sure you have the time to do this.

Carol Ann Johnson.

RETIRED GREYHOUNDS

There are two categories of rescued dogs that do not fit the normal pattern because of the circumstances by which they become in need of new homes. These are retired racing Greyhounds and American Pit Bull Terriers. Because of the extraordinary legal tangle which surrounds the Pit Bull, these dogs are dealt with in Chapter 7: Dogs and the Law. Greyhounds, however, are a breed that merits your consideration if you are attracted to a dog of this type.

Like most dogs, Greyhounds have a life span of ten or more years, but their racing life probably ends after four to six years. It may be very much shorter – as little as fifteen months – if a dog does not fulfil its original promise. As a result, there are Greyhounds looking for homes at a variety of ages from fifteen months onwards, although the majority are about four years of age.

Greyhounds are large dogs and require a reasonable amount of space in the home. Their basic temperament is gentle, and they can become friendly, loving companions. Before retirement, racing Greyhounds lead a curious and sheltered life. For a start, they virtually never see any breed other than their own – and they may be frightened or aggressive when first meeting another breed. However, the opposite applies to their attitude to humans. For the whole of their lives, they have been used to meeting a large number of different people. One evening's racing means that they are probably handled by as many as eight, some of them complete strangers. They are used to the blaze of the lights and the roar of the crowd. Put a lead on a Greyhound and it will happily trot off with you. This does not mean that it will not eventually develop a close relationship with one person. The more time you spend together the closer you become. The Greyhound has been bred for centuries to pursue and catch small animals. You must be aware of this, and take the necessary precautions. It is not the dog's fault if you let him loose in the park and he immediately takes off after a cat or small dog. Until you are certain that you have restrained that instinct, your Greyhound should always be on a lead and wearing a wire muzzle when in a public place. Once he realises that there are other creatures in the world, he will learn to accept them and take his place in the family.

SUMMARY

For anyone deciding to take on a rescued dog there is an enormous choice. There are dogs sitting in rescue kennels of every size, shape and character. While you, on your side, will have a choice, the dog will be content with whatever fate brings. Humans will always wish to make changes to any thing or person that they are associated with. The dog will accept you as you are – rich or poor, fat or thin, young or old. From the tramp's mongrel to the Royal Corgi, the dog is content with the human that he agrees to call his master.

Whatever you choose, you can be almost sure that, given your patience and love, your dog will become a wonderful friend and companion. Together you will become another example of the goodness and decency of dog ownership.

Chapter Two
THE RESCUERS

There are a very large number of organisations and individuals working to rescue and rehabilitate lost, unwanted and ill-used dogs. It is debatable whether this indicates our great love of dogs or the opposite. Whichever is the answer, dogs can be thankful that there are many people who are prepared to devote a large part of their lives, and a large part of their income, to their welfare.

THE ORGANISATIONS
Welfare organisations vary enormously in size, facilities and concept. The large, national, welfare bodies have funds running into millions of pounds, extensive purpose-built kennels, well-organised publicity machines, and highly trained and dedicated staff. At the other end of the scale, there are the small, private rescue kennels often operated in the back garden by one or two devoted dog lovers. In addition to the bodies dealing with the rescue of all dogs, there are breed rescue organisations working for the welfare of particular breeds. Virtually every breed has its own rescue body, supported by funds raised by its breed clubs.

All welfare bodies rely on donations, collecting boxes and other fundraising schemes. No welfare organisation receives any government support, although some of the larger ones are undertaking contract work for local government services involved in animal welfare as a source of extra income – an approach which combines the expertise of the welfare body with its financial needs. In the small rescue kennels, one or two people, often a husband and wife team, combine all the duties, including organiser, kennelmaid, collector of dogs, fundraiser, interviewer of prospective new owners, and dog psychologist.

Sadly, none of these rescue efforts are superfluous. Almost all rescue bodies are struggling to cope with large numbers of dogs needing their care. Figures for dogs destroyed are both revealing and sad. Many of the breed rescue societies show that they destroy less than one per cent of dogs taken into care. These are the cases where a dog is of such a nature that it would be foolish to put him back in the community, or because his physical condition is so bad that the kindest thing is to put him down. At the other end of the picture, the RSPCA statistics show that in the region of fifty per cent of the dogs that come into their hands are destroyed. Suprisingly, the local government dog wardens whose mandate is to enforce the law, rather than to act as a charity, show a figure of less than thirty per cent. Most other major charities dealing with all breeds show very much lower destruction figures – twenty per cent or less. You may think that the most common reason for a dog being destroyed is because it has bitten someone or misbehaved in some other way. Actually, in the majority of cases, the crime for which a dog receives the death sentence is that it has been abandoned, lost or thrown out by its owner, and no other person can be found to take responsibility for it. Furthermore, although most rescue organisations do not take advantage of it, the law allows the dog to be destroyed if there is no claimant for it after seven days.

Most of the rescue organisations work to a similar code of practice. A large proportion of them, including breed rescue, are registered charities. The paramount interest is for the welfare of the dog. This is achieved by caring for and rehabilitating the dogs that come into their care, and, hopefully, finding new homes. If it is not possible to rehome a dog, then most organisations will keep it for as long as possible, and some bodies will keep the dog for its natural life if no home can be found. Wherever possible, the proposed home will be visited, with follow-up visits to check that the dog is settled in with its new family.

In many cases, dogs are spayed or neutered before being rehomed. Alternatively, the person adopting the dog may have to sign an undertaking to have this carried out. It is usual for the rescue organisations to retain the legal ownership of the dog so that they can reclaim the dog if the new home fails to be satisfactory in any way. For this reason, no charge is made for the dog as such, but a donation towards the costs is expected.

As a general rule, if your interest is in acquiring a pure-bred dog, then your approach should be made to the relevant breed rescue body, although pure-bred dogs make up a sizeable proportion (over twenty per cent) in all rescue kennels shelters. If you have no special preference or are a mongrel supporter, then go to an all-breed rescue kennel. We have learnt in our visits to a large number of people who have given homes to mongrels what wonderful companions they can be. Some of the shelters also take in other unwanted animals. Many take in cats and guinea pigs, fox cubs, hedgehogs and other species. Staff at a Wood Green Shelter tell the story of a man who arrived to offer a home to 'the baby hippopotamus'. This caused some confusion as they were quite sure that they did not have a hippopotamus. The caller insisted that they did and that his friend had seen it the previous day. He had driven a long distance in great haste as he had always wanted one. Eventually they traced the hippo: one very black and muddy Vietnamese Pot-Bellied pig!

THE DOGS' HOME BATTERSEA
If you say "dog show" to the average man in the street, he will say "Crufts",

and will probably be totally unaware that Crufts is only one of dozens of major dog shows held each year. Equally, if you say "dogs' home" to the same man, he will almost certainly say "Battersea", although it is only one of the many bodies working for their welfare. However, it is fair to say that Battersea established the pattern which has been followed by many other institutions, not only in Britain but in many other parts of the world.

The Dogs' Home Battersea was founded in 1860 as The Temporary Home for Lost or Starving Dogs. Starting life in Islington, it moved to Battersea in 1871. Dogs, lost, starving and abused, have continued to pour through its doors ever since. At the time of writing, Battersea deals with between 14,000 and 20,000 dogs per year. Since its foundation some three million dogs have found refuge there. Battersea was founded by a woman, Mary Tealby, who decided that something had to be done about the stray dogs roaming the streets of London. She and a group of like-minded friends started to take the strays into their homes, fed them, cared for them and, if possible, found them new homes. In the typical way that so many of our famous institutions were founded in Victorian times, the idea was taken up by a committee of gentlemen, and Battersea was established. In 1879 the then Prince of Wales made a tour of Battersea. Five years later the youngest son of Queen Victoria, Prince Leopold, not only made a visit but adopted a small terrier called Skippy. Queen Victoria approved, and in 1888 she became Patron. In 1956 Her Majesty Queen Elizabeth II agreed to take up the same appointment.

Battersea is very noisy, crowded, and heartbreaking. Packed into a cramped area under the railway arches are the unwanted and lost dogs of London and the surrounding area. Space is at such a premium that some of the kennels are on three floors. Apart from taking the daily collection of dogs picked up by the police and local authorities, it also provides temporary homes for the dogs of prisoners, and for those who are in hospital and unable to provide for their dogs. Very sensibly, Battersea has now acquired a country annex located in spacious grounds at Bellmead, just outside Windsor, where dogs can be rehabilitated under ideal conditions.

Many owners, when asked why they chose their dog, answer: "We didn't choose him, he chose us." The dog had singled them out and made it clear that he liked them. A member of staff commented on this when we were visiting Bellmead, and we found it was a view shared by many welfare workers and owners of rescued dogs. Conversely, dogs repeatedly make it clear that they do not like certain people. A German Shorthaired Pointer refused to settle in four different homes. None of them lasted more than forty-eight hours, although there were no obvious reasons for his dislike. In the fifth home, the dog settled immediately and has been happy there ever since.

Unlike the majority of welfare organisations, Battersea actually sells the dogs that it rehomes. The price is about £70 at present. They argue that purchase gives a sense of responsibility to the new owner, and, bearing in mind that this charge includes neutering, it can hardly be called excessive. Battersea does a difficult job and does it well. Its inmates are literally picked up from the gutter, and every type of problem dog files through its gates every day. It has become as much a part of the London scene as Tower Bridge and Trafalgar Square – even the dogs seem to have a streetwise Cockney air about them.

WOOD GREEN ANIMAL SHELTER

The routine for accepting, rehabilitating and rehoming a dog coming into a rescue kennel inevitably depends on the resources and size of the organisation. For the small rescue kennel running on a tight financial budget and a lot of love, the new arrival probably gets a bath, a good meal, a warm bed and a cuddle. The dog almost certainly finds this quite adequate, and the wonderful work done by this type of rescue kennel is not to be decried. With the large organisations, the numbers of dogs passing through the system make it essential that a set routine is followed both as a means of administration and for the welfare of the dog.

As a part of our research for this book, we decided to follow a dog through the system from the time of its arrival at the rescue kennels until it went to its new owner, and to then look at its life and progress in its new home. This also seemed a good way of looking at the organisation, its problems and achievements. Different organisations have varying systems, but the final aim is the same for all of them: to place a healthy dog in a happy and loving home.

Kennel blocks at Wood Green Animal Shelters, in Godmanchester.

We chose to make our study at the Wood Green Animal Shelter, at Godmanchester, as an excellent example of a modern, purpose-built rescue kennels. During the time we spent there we found that we were not only recording the progress of our chosen dog but we were also gaining an insight into the daily round of tragedies and not a few comedies that make up life at the Shelter.

For a rescued dog life begins anew at the Animal Reception Centre. Here, in a small office, complete with a computer terminal and a couple of chairs for visitors, incoming dogs are processed into the system. Although this sounds a slightly cold-blooded description, in fact, we found from our first contact that the Shelter staff are, without exception, caring, knowledgeable and compassionate animal lovers whose expertise covers not only animals but also human behaviour. The receptionist needs to obtain the fullest possible picture of the dog. As far as possible, she will record on the computer all the relevant details about its history, behaviour and likes and dislikes. Ideally, the receptionist wants to know:

1. Will the dog mix with other dogs or cats?
2. Is it used to children?
3. How much exercise does it get?
4. Is it used to riding in a car?
5. How often is it fed, and what has it been fed on?
6. Is it used to being left alone at home?
7. How long has the dog been with its present owner?

The receptionist will also check the dog's reaction to herself, recording whether it is nervous, bold, friendly or aggressive. Proof must be obtained regarding the ownership of the dog. It can happen that the person who brings in a dog is the dog-hating half of a relationship taking advantage of their partner's temporary absence to get rid of the dog. One visitor to a rescue kennel recognised the dog that her estranged husband claimed to have had put down two years previously. Not only that, but the dog recognised her, and was delighted to be taken back home again!

Those who bring their dogs to the shelter do so for all sorts of reasons, some of which can colour their description of the dog's character and behaviour. Many are heartbroken at having to give up a beloved pet because of reasons beyond their control. Understandably, their chief concern is that the dog should go to a home where it will be happy and well looked after, and the dog's many virtues are given at great length.

Other owners have decided that they do not want a dog, or they do not want *that* dog. These owners tend to give a long catalogue of the dog's sins as their reason for getting rid of it, some of which sound rather unlikely when you look at the dog sitting trustfully by their side. Whatever the reasons, true or false, for the dog coming to the Shelter, it will be taken in and cared for.

SADIE'S CASE HISTORY

It was April when Sadie, arrived at the Shelter. She had no owner to tell us her history, or who she was. She was brought in by a dog warden, who had been contacted by the Cambridge police. She had been found wandering in the streets, and she hardly looked like the beauty that she was to become later. She was very thin and underweight, her long coat was dirty and matted, and she was suffering from kennel cough. The kennel staff soon named her "the doormat on four legs". At a guess, she was about seven to eight months of age. She may well have been a pretty, fluffy puppy given as a Christmas present, and then thrown out when the owner got bored with her.

Sadie rated friendly and submissive on the receptionist's assessment. She was issued with an identity disc and allotted a number, and she was then weighed so that her weight could be monitored while she was in the Shelter. The next stop was the veterinary surgery. The Shelter has a staff of three veterinary surgeons and eight veterinary nurses. With the large number of dog and cats, not to mention other animals dealt with by the Shelter, they are kept busy. The Shelter has a policy of spaying all bitches before they are rehomed, and this

Sadie, rehomed from Wood Green Animal Shelters, now a happy, lively member of her new family.

means an average of three spaying operations per day. At this stage, Sadie was given a general health-check including eyes, ears, teeth, paws and coat. She was vaccinated and wormed and a veterinary record completed. Again, her reaction to the veterinary handling and grooming was recorded, confirming the assessment of the receptionist.

The next stage was a spell in a separate kennel in one of the isolation blocks. These are designed so that the dog can see all that is going on, but avoids any physical contact with other dogs. The aim is to prevent any cross-infection from a dog who may be incubating a disease when it comes into the Shelter, and also to reduce the stress factor which could occur if a new dog was suddenly thrust into a pen of other dogs. The walk to the isolation block was the first opportunity to see how Sadie reacted to walking on a lead, and so her reaction was again recorded. Some dogs show fear and resistance to being led off on a lead, but after an initial tug in the wrong direction, Sadie trotted off quite happily.

She spent a week in the isolation block, and she was continuously assessed by the kennel staff. This assessment included:

1. Was she was clean in her kennel?
2. Was she destructive?
3. Were her motions normal?
4. Was she a good or a poor feeder?
5. Did she show any reactions to basic commands such as "Sit", "Down" or "Heel"?

Sadie produced no particular surprises or problems during her assessment period. Her "house-training" was not perfect, she showed no signs of previous training, and her appetite was not enormous, but satisfactory. However, the staff have to be vigilant for problems which may arise during this critical period of assessment. The staff tell a story of a Bullmastiff, kennelled in isolation, who passed perfectly normal motions – except that they frequently contained coins ranging from single pennies to a 50 pence piece. For a few days, it looked as if they had the canine equivalent of the goose that laid the golden eggs. However, the money supply stopped after reaching £2.53 pence. Perhaps the final misdeed that landed the dog in the Shelter was eating its owner's paypacket!

At this stage we can introduce Joy Leach, who is now Sadie's 'owner', although the term 'keeper' is more accurate. Although for all practical purposes the person who takes a rescue dog into their home is the owner, Wood Green retains the legal ownership of the dog. This precaution is for the welfare of the dog, so that in the unlikely event of the rehoming being unsuitable, the dog can be taken back to the protection of the Shelter. This also applies if the 'keeper' is unable to continue to give a home to the dog. Although Joy had owned five dogs before and during the early years of her marriage, there was a twelve-year gap without dogs while she was busy bringing up a family. However, the household was not without animals during this time. There were several cats, a rabbit, a hamster and goldfish.

After her spell in isolation, Sadie was moved into one of the main runs with other dogs looking for new homes. Her general assessment was that she was suitable for adoption. This happened to be the day that Joy made a trip to Wood Green. At first, the trip did not seem to be very successful – nothing caught Joy's eye. However, just as she was about to leave, she looked over the half-door of one of the kennels and there was this small, hairy, rather subdued little dog. One of the problems of visiting the Shelter is that almost every dog has an appealing look in its eyes which just begs you to take it home. This one certainly had that effect on Joy and she put a reserve on her. We are not sure who considers themselves the luckiest – Joy for choosing Sadie before anyone else was able to do so, or Sadie for finding a loving home within hours of being put in the general pen.

However, adoption is not just a question of picking up your chosen dog and going home with it. Wood Green likes to meet the whole family and visit the home before passing on a dog. In Joy's case, there was no problem with the family, but the Shelter visitor suggested that more fencing was required to make the garden secure. Because Joy's family included cats it was arranged for Sadie's reaction to cats to be tested at the Shelter. She passed this test successfully, but she was probably on her best behaviour as she is still not very keen on Joy's cats. Sadie also had to be spayed and this was done on April 22nd. The following day Sadie started her new life with Joy and her family.

Sadie got her name after Joy and her family decided that she was a bit of an old-fashioned girl. In fact, it has been suggested that she has ambitions to be considered a lady rather than the tomboy she appears to be. She settled in quickly. One of her few sins was to chew up the sun-lounger, spreading the stuffing all over the garden. Although not completely house-trained on arrival, she soon learnt the proper procedure. She showed an interest in gardening, which she still retains, digging up any plants which she considers to be in the wrong place. She enjoys riding in the car which has been changed from a saloon to a hatchback for her convenience, and she is an enthusiastic caravaner.

Joy was not content to have a dog that would just spend her time eating, sleeping, going for walks, and making sure that the cats do not get too big for their paws. Sadie is a regular student at the weekly training classes run by Wood Green, and she is a member of the agility demonstration team. Sadie has proved both her ability and beauty by winning a large collection of rosettes for obedience, and competing in exemption shows, which are held for charity. Probably the highlight of her career so far was to be runner-up in the final of the Rescue Dog of the Year, competing against four thousand rescued dogs for the award.

Sadie greeted us at the door when we went back to see her. She gravely gave us a paw to shake and then brought her favourite squeaky toy for our approval. When the postman arrived she collected the letters from the mat and brought them to Joy. Sadie likes to keep an eye on the world, and she has a favourite hole in the fence for observing the neighbours' kittens, and she uses the cat-flap to watch for visitors. Although she sleeps in a basket in the kitchen, she is not averse to dragging her rug over Joy's lap before climbing up for a rest.

We were told that she still has a few more ambitions: one is to run in the London Marathon with Joy's husband, Martin; another is to curl up next to the family cat without being hissed at. Sadie is a success. Although this is the result of the love and care given her by Joy and her family, Sadie herself has made her own contribution by her happy, friendly and trusting attitude to humans and the world in general. In Joy's words: "She has enhanced our lives. We are all fitter, happier people by having her. She makes many friends by bringing out the best in the people she meets."

SMALL RESCUE GROUPS

A recent welfare development is the rescue group. These usually consist of a number of people working together for the welfare of dogs and other animals in a particular area. Such groups are not registered as charities and rely for their funding on their own efforts. Most groups do not have their own kennel accommodation and use local boarding kennels often at special low rates. Such groups are often drawn from members of dog training clubs, who use their personal experience and expertise.

There is usually no formal organisation; members believe that it is more important to spend the time and money that is available on the welfare of the animals, rather than on administration. These groups are often built around a few natural organisers, who, if they were not working for animals, would be involved in some other form of charity. Each person contributes what they can either in the form of fundraising or actually working with the dogs. A typical animal rescue group consists of some twelve to fifteen workers, with roughly half engaged in raising money and the remainder working with the dogs. Their monthly kennel bill amounts to about £600, so the fundraisers are kept busy.

The group tries to deal with problems of dog-owning before they become terminal by offering advice and guidance to owners, in the hope that they can solve the difficulty before the owner gives up and discards the dog. The obedience training experience of the advisors is therefore invaluable Their knowledge is also used for the assessment of dogs that they are holding in kennels and of the suitability of proposed new homes, and for follow-up visits to rehomed dogs. This type of rescue group is often used by the police and local dog warden when the need arises. As with so many workers in welfare, the members find themselves involved with many tragic cases. There is certainly no financial benefit to be gained: far from it – the work invariably costs them money. The organiser of one group summed up their objectives with the comment: " We are in it for the animals."

BREED CLUB RESCUE

With the large number of breed rescue organisations, it was obviously impossible for us to look at all of them. We decided to look at the Yorkshire Terrier Club Rescue for three reasons: firstly because the breed is one of the most popular in Britain, and we have found that popularity leads to problems; secondly, because the Yorkie is one of the smallest breeds of dog. The combination of popularity and small size makes the breed attractive to commercial breeders, who are producing stock solely for profit, with little regard to the future welfare of the dogs that they sell. Our third reason for choosing the Yorkie is because the breed has a special place in our hearts.

Yorkshire Terrier Rescue and Re-Homing, to give it its full title, covers the entire country and is controlled by Mrs Beryl Evans from a pleasant house in a suburb of Bedford. From here, the network of area representatives is co-ordinated so that a dog in need of help can be quickly taken into the system and, hopefully, found a new home. Sensibly, they have an arrangement with the major "all breed" welfare shelters that any Yorkies coming into their kennels are passed on to the YTC Rescue. The house is easy to find. As you approach the front door you are greeted by a chorus of high-pitched barks. It is slightly confusing when you realise that some of these come from the house next-door, until Mrs Evans explains that her next-door neighbours help her by providing temporary foster homes.

Although the fact that dogs need help can never be dismissed lightly, the situation with Yorkies is not unsatisfactory. YTC Rescue rehomes about 400 dogs per year. This has to be compared with the total number bred, which is in excess of 20,000 per year. On average, only two dogs per year are put down as being impossible to place in new homes. The success rate for rehoming is therefore almost 100 per cent – a rate that many breed rescue organisations would envy. Other breeds would also be envious of the waiting list of prospective owners which runs at 1500 to 2000 at any one time.

Only a small numbers of Yorkies coming into Rescue are actually strays, as opposed to dogs that are handed over by their previous owners. One little stray bitch had been living on a building site and had been fed by the building workers. As they were all going home for Christmas, they very sensibly handed her over to Rescue. In common with almost all rescue workers, Mrs Evans finds that there are a small percentage of dogs in the system that are virtually impossible to rehome. The old, those traumatised by past ill-treatment, or those temperamentally impossible to pass on to another home, come into this category. These dogs will spend the rest of their lives being cared for by her.

Tina was one of five worn-out brood bitches who were left tied up outside a supermarket with a notice saying "Help yourself". The bitches had obviously been discarded after being bred from at every season until they were worn-out and exhausted. Of the others, one had already been taken, two had died, and one was found a home; Tina was taken in by Mrs Evans. Her teats were huge from feeding an endless stream of puppies, and she had an enormous hernia. She could only be described as a zombie. She made no response whatsoever to any attempt to approach or talk to her, and she fled to a hiding-place in the garden hedge, where she lived for months. Fortunately it was summer and the weather was warm. The only time she would eat was at night when she would creep through the open sun-lounge door and gulp down the food left there for her. The hernia was operated on, but it was so severe that it could only be partially cured. All this was five years ago. Tina will now come into the house, but she still dislikes strangers and is terrified of noise. When she is picked up, you can see the fear in her eyes but at least she now accepts that she has a home and safety.

Being small, cuddly, pretty and extrovert, the Yorkie excels as companion and therapeutic aid to the disabled and elderly. Rescue Yorkies have become successful companions to patients recovering from strokes, to a sufferer from spina bifida and as a much-loved pet in old people's homes. Nelson was booked to go to a home for elderly ladies. The warden asked whether some of the residents could come to collect him. On the appointed day, the warden arrived in a minibus containing no less than nine ladies, complete with walking frames. Mrs Evans responded magnificently, providing tea and biscuits and introducing them to the dogs. "The only problem was when they all wanted to use the rather small lavatory before leaving," she said. "There was a queue of walking frames all through the house!" Eventually the minibus was reloaded and drove off with the addition of Nelson, happily looking out of the window, together with his nine ladies.

THE 'ONE-MAN BAND'

We looked at the highly organised national set-ups, and we looked at the breed club rescue kennels. Both have some sort of financial support from the general public or from their breed clubs. We then visited some of the privately owned kennels, run by people whose motivation is a love of dogs and the determination to do what they can to help them.

After several miles of winding Suffolk lanes and a mile of rough farm track, we came to a small farm house and some rather dilapidated buildings. This is Winsey Farm, famous in the area as a home for unwanted animals of all kinds, but in particular as a refuge for dogs. Run by Leah and Harry Lovett, this is a rescue kennel which has on the credit side of its balance sheet an asset which is rarely taken into account by dog welfare bodies. The Lovetts have a devout trust in God and believe that all his creatures deserve our love and care. Listening to them talking about their efforts you get the feeling that at times there is little else, other than their belief, to help them cope with the task they have set themselves. Both of them are in their mid-seventies and have been rescuing dogs for thirty-five years.

We were greeted at the gate by Leah and at least six small dogs, all of whom were determined to join us indoors. Four succeeded and immediately climbed on our laps and settled down to sleep. The combined ages of the four came to something like forty-five years, and each had a story behind them. One had arrived as a puppy, so covered by dermodectic mange that the vet had suggested that the dog should be put down. Leah cured the mange, and the dog was still going strong twelve years later. One bitch had only three legs. While she was in whelp, the bitch had been kicked and her leg had been broken. The owner refused to have the leg attended to. Eventually Leah rescued the bitch, by which time the leg was septic and had to be amputated. In spite of this she had her puppies, reared them, and was still with Leah ten years later.

The Lovetts did not set out to have a rescue kennel – they started with a boarding kennel. However, the second boarder that they had was not wanted by his owner and he stayed on. Very quickly, the rescued dogs began to out-number the boarders – and that is the way it has continued for the last thirty-five years. Money is a perpetual problem. No dogs are sold, but those who provide homes are asked for a donation. Many of the animals, including a fox, a cockatoo, and a donkey, stay with the Lovetts for the whole of their lives – and all need to be fed. Local tradespeople help. The baker makes a regular contribution of leftover food. Steak pies and sausage rolls have their meat content removed to feed the dogs, while the pastry goes to feed the chickens, whose thirty or so eggs per day are cooked and included in the dog food. The local roads and lanes provide a steady supply of run-over rabbits and pheasants, which, provided they are not too damaged, give a source of meat for the dogs, with the remainder of the carcase feeding the fox and the ferrets. One year produced a Christmas bonus when a local farmer donated a whole stag which had to be destroyed after injuring itself on a barbed wire fence during a storm. The local vets, and Cambridge University Veterinary College help with veterinary treatment. On the debit side, although the local Social Services seek her help with dogs belonging to their clients, they make no attempt to pay her for her assistance.

Leah considers that prayer solves many of their problems. She tells the story of a telephone-call on the day before Christmas asking her to take in a Westie bitch. The owner was going away for Christmas; she was not prepared to pay for the Westie to go into a boarding kennels for the holiday, neither would she arrange for her to be delivered to the Lovetts. If Leah would not come and collect the bitch, the woman threatened that she would tell her son to put the bitch down. If she wanted a dog after her return from holiday, she would buy another. Leah had neither kennel space nor transport, but she begged the owner to give her a few hours while she tried to sort something out. Leah's prayers were answered. An hour later she had a very tearful telephone-call from a lady to say that her beloved Westie had just died, and she did not know how she would get through Christmas alone without the company of her dog. She was given the Westie's address and instructed to say that she was collecting for Leah – and a happy Christmas for the Westie bitch and her new owner followed. The story has a sequel. On her return from holiday, the original owner asked for her dog back. She got a very dusty answer.

Although Winsey Farm is a very different set-up from the large animal welfare organisations, it plays just as vital a part in rehoming dogs. At the end of term a school teacher looked at the cage of mice kept by the class and said: "Who has a cat at home?" Five children put up their hands. "Right," said the teacher, "you can each have a mouse to take home for your cat." One tearful small boy told his parents, and the mice were saved. Inevitably, one of the mice finished up with the Lovetts. "We suppose you gave it a home," we said. "Oh yes", said Leah, "it's a dear little thing and lives in its cage on the kitchen mantlepiece." The Lovetts have a slogan: they "never say no" to an animal in need. A lot of dogs would be a lot worse off without them.

Chapter Three
LIVING WITH A RESCUED DOG

The pleasure of owning a dog can be made or marred by the amount of thought and effort that you put into looking after his welfare, understanding him, training him, and generally establishing a good relationship with him.

Training is dealt with in Chapter 5. In this chapter we concentrate on general care, starting with the moment when you collect your dog from the rescue kennels.

COLLECTING YOUR DOG
When you collect your rescued dog, he may already have some sort of collar and lead. If he does, take a good look at both the collar and the lead while you are still within the security of the kennel. The fact that the dog was unwanted by his previous owner probably means that they were unwilling to spend money on good, strong equipment. You may find that both the collar and the lead are worn and frayed and even tied up with string.

These may have been adequate when the dog was with an owner that he knew, but he is now about to be led away into an unknown future by a stranger. The dog is likely to try and pull away from you, and if he escapes into a crowded road you will have little chance of recapturing him – and yet another stray dog hits the streets.

For your rescued dog, we suggest a good-quality leather collar of a size that fits closely around the neck. You should just be able to slip a finger inside the collar, without undue discomfort to the dog. Do not have it too loose or the dog will either pull it over his head with his paws, or back out of it. The collar should be comfortable enough for the dog to wear all the time – not just when you take him out. This means that if your dog ever escapes, he is easier to catch, and he will also be wearing his identification disc (see below).

With the collar, you should use a flat, leather lead of a strength suitable for the size of the dog. It is preferable to have a fairly long lead, which you can shorten by wrapping around your fist, thus giving you a certain amount of flexibility as to its length in varying circumstances. Make sure that the lead clip is of good quality – the cheap, bent tin ones will fail at the crucial moment. Nylon leads will cut into your hand if the dog pulls.

THE JOURNEY HOME

Having got your dog secured on his collar and lead as you leave the rescue kennels, you are now ready to take him home. This journey will probably be made in your car. Remember that you are a stranger to the dog. Your car is a strange place and the dog is probably frightened. It is advisable to take a companion to sit with, or hold the dog during the journey. If you have a small dog, it may be worthwhile to borrow a cage for the journey.

Much as the children may wish to come and collect their new friend, it is probably better that you leave them at home on this occasion. You cannot be certain how the dog will behave, and if he becomes frightened or aggressive, the back of a moving car, full of children is no place for it to happen. An old "dog person's" trick is to shut the last six inches of the lead in the door, so that it hangs outside. In this way, you can be holding the lead before you open the door, thus preventing the mad dash for freedom which the dog may attempt when you arrive home.

ARRIVING HOME

Before taking on a rescued dog, you should ensure that your garden is secure so that a dog cannot possibly escape. Most dogs will soon learn the limits of their territory, but they will enlarge this if it is physically possible to do so. Some dogs have no difficulty jumping over a six foot fence, but this does not mean you have to turn your garden into a fortress. For the determined escaper, a small run complete with a roof will give security, while the rest of the garden can be used under supervision.

A sensible approach to fencing is to use chain-link to a height of 5-6ft. The bottom six inches can be sunk into the ground, and it is a good idea to run a path of concrete or paving stones along the bottom of the fence, in order to prevent digging and wear of the grass. The dog should be confined to the back garden, thus allowing free access for the postman, milkman and other visitors.

The day your rescued dog arrives should not be the occasion for a welcome-home party of family, relations and friends. The occasion will be traumatic enough for the dog without having to cope with a crowd of strange people. Give the dog a chance to explore and to accept his new home. If you have children, brief them not to make loud noises and sudden movements, and allow the dog to get to know them in his own time, rather than being smothered and frightened with misplaced kindness. Do not allow your children to be over-enthusiastic about taking the new arrival out and playing with him. The dog, especially if he is a youngster, will require his ration of sleep, and you should not allow him to be constantly dragged out of his bed for yet another game.

If you already have another pet, make sure the introduction takes place under your supervision. If you already have a dog, it is advisable to make the introduction on neutral ground – such as at the park – so that there is no question of an invasion of territory. If you own a cat, make sure the first meeting is controlled, so that the pair get off on the right footing. The established pet, especially if it is a dog, should be given extra love and attention during the introductory period. Nothing is more likely to cause trouble than jealousy, because your old and faithful companion feels he has lost his place to a young intruder.

THE FIRST MEAL

Your first reaction when you get your rescued dog home will probably be to give him a large and tasty meal, both to compensate for previous deprivation and to show him that, with you, life will be better. It is highly likely that the result of your kindness will be that your new dog develops violent diarrhoea, to the detriment of your relationship with him – and to your carpet. Sudden change in a dog's diet, or an increase in volume, can upset a dog's stomach, as can the trauma of changing homes. Treatment for diarrhoea is covered in Chapter 6, Health Care, but it is obviously better to try to avoid the condition, which is easily started but more difficult to cure. If your dog has been in rescue kennels for some time, the staff will be able to tell you what diet they have been feeding; they may even give you a couple of days supply. At all events, feed small quantities until your dog has settled down. (Feeding and Nutrition is covered in detail in Chapter 4.)

SLEEPING QUARTERS

Some dogs, especially small ones, will decide that you are their bed, and they will try to snuggle up as close as possible. When you go to bed, the dog will join you. When you settle in your favourite armchair, the dog will tuck himself alongside you. Happiness for such a dog is mainly found in close contact with the person that he loves, and who loves and looks after him in return. There is much to be said for this kind of relationship. The more time that the two of you spend together, the closer the understanding between you.

We owned a much-loved Yorkshire Terrier who always slept on the bed. Occasionally, during the night he would hop off the bed, stretch his legs and jump back up again. This worked very well until old age and heart trouble started to slow him down. We would then be woken up in the small hours by a steady thumping, as he repeatedly tried and failed to jump back on the bed. Not only were we woken up, but we were also worried that he would give himself a heart attack. Wearily, one of us would reach out, and groping in the dark, lift him back up. Eventually there was only one action we could take. We cut the legs off the bed. The alternative was to sleep on the floor. Not everyone is prepared to be quite so besotted with their dog!

For the dog's own confidence and sense of security, he needs to have a bed that he can call his own. Somewhere that he can retire to at night, when he feels like a snooze, or when his owner tells him to get out of the way. Where you decide that this should be must depend on your domestic arrangements. There are advantages in being able to shut the dog away from the main part of the house when you are doing the vacuum cleaning, or when visitors call. At the same time, if you are going to form a close relationship with your dog, you need to spend as much time with him as possible. This means that under the kitchen table is probably the best location for the dog bed. You can shut the door on the dog when you want to, and if the dog is under the table, he has a private place which will give him a sense of security – and you will not be falling over him all the time!

For a medium to large dog, or for a dog that looks like being destructive if left alone in the house, it is worth considering a kennel and small run in the garden. This does not mean that your dog should live permanently in a kennel. The kennel should be used as a place of safety when you are out, or when you do not want the dog in the house. The disadvantage of an outdoor kennel, particularly if you have close neighbours, is that the dog may spend his time barking at the next door cat and generally creating a nuisance.

For a small dog, the alternative to an outdoor kennel is a large weldmesh cage, placed in a convenient corner indoors. Such a cage needs to be of sufficient size for the dog to stand at his full height, and to be able to turn round and lie full length. The advantage of using a weldmesh cage is that the dog can see and hear all the family activity that is going on around him. Cages are used by many dog breeders as a place to rear a puppy, accustoming the pup to domestic sights and sounds. Frequently the dog will continue to use the cage as his bed, even when the door is left open.

However, the kennel or cage should only be used for short periods at a time. Under no circumstances should you use an old-fashioned yard chain to fasten your dog in the garden. The dog will probably be inadequately protected against the weather, and he will spend his time pulling on the chain, barking and defending his territory.

BEDS AND BEDDING

A dog bed which provides some side shelter from draughts, holds the bedding together, and allows the dog a place to store his favourite toys is essential. We do not recommend the old-fashioned woven wicker-basket. A bored dog will while away the odd lonely hour chewing at the wicker-work, and we have seen many examples of this type of basket which have been reduced to a flat disc, all the sides having been chewed away. The oval-shaped fibre glass beds are fairly resistant to chewing and easy to keep clean. If your dog is still growing, make sure that you buy a bed large enough for him as an adult. If you are starting with a puppy who has a lot of growing to do, then it is probably better to use cardboard boxes which can easily be replaced until the pup is old enough to graduate to a proper bed.

Your dog needs bed clothes as well as a bed. For this, you can use several layers of newspaper as a lining, with an old blanket, folded several times, placed on top. When your dog first arrives at your home, feelings of stress and anxiety may result in the dog ripping his blanket to pieces. For this reason, it is advisable to use an old blanket, or even disused curtains or a piece of carpet. Nothing can be worse for your mutual relationship than to find that expensive new blanket, specially purchased for your dog's comfort, torn into three inch squares. Provided that the torn up bits provide some sort of padding, you should leave them there. Maybe that's the way that the dog wants it.

The blanket will need washing occasionally – not too often as dogs like their own familiar smell. Dog hairs may give you a problem with the filters in your washing machine, so that you may find it better to wash the blanket by hand. You may be tempted to provide a little extra comfort by providing an old pillow or cushion. If you do, make sure that the filling is not small feathers or down. If your dog decides to find out what is inside the pillow, you will come back one day to a heap of feathers with a nose and ears sticking out! You will then spend the next few weeks chasing feathers from odd corners of the house. The same applies to the 'bean bag' type of dog bed. Dogs like them and find them comfortable, but if the tiny pea-like filling escapes from the bag, you will be finding them all over the place.

DISHES AND BOWLS
You will need a drinking-water bowl and a food dish, as it is still preferable to have special dishes allocated to the dog so that he knows which is his dish. Plastic dishes designed for dogs are cheap and effective. The only disadvantage is that their lightness allows them to slide around the floor, and the dog has to chase his dinner under the table. Bowls made of heavy brown china look attractive, but if you have one of those dogs who brings you his dish as a reminder that it is dinner time, you will find that it will break when dropped on a hard surface. The best type to use are those made of stainless steel, which are easy to wash and last a lifetime.

TOYS
As with proprietary pet foods, many of the toys which you can buy are designed to appeal to you rather than your dog. Watching your dog chew the nose off a plastic model of your least favourite politician may give you pleasure. It is doubtful whether your dog will appreciate how much you paid for the toy, and the dog would probably be just as happy with one of your old socks.

Dogs, like children, are often happiest with something which is cheap and simple – cardboard boxes are always enjoyed. Most dogs will enjoy chasing after a stick, but this is not to be recommended because sharp twigs could splinter off and stick in your dog's throat, and eyes could also be at risk.

If you buy toys, then the best type are the hard, rubber balls, bones or other shapes. They will stand a considerable amount of chewing and can be thrown

Pet shops offer a wide range of dog beds. The most durable is the kidney-shaped fibre-glass bed (pictured centre), lined with a blanket or some other type of bedding.

Steve Nash.

Your dog will need a feeding bowl and a drinking bowl. The stainless-steel type are easy to clean and last a lifetime.

Steve Nash.

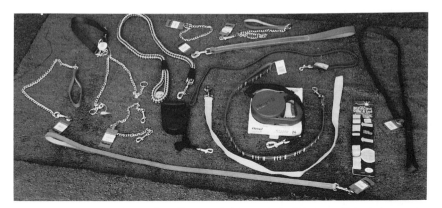

*A good-quality leather lead, with a trigger hook (picture above) is strong
and reliable. An extension lead is also a useful item of equipment.*

Steve Nash

*If you are buying
toys for your dog,
make sure you
choose items
which are tough
and cannot be
chewed into small
bits which could
be dangerous if
swallowed.
Steve Nash.*

for the dog to retrieve. Balls must be large enough to prevent the dog getting
the ball stuck in his throat. It is all too easy for the dog to chase a small ball,
swallow it in his excitement, and then choke on it. Even for a small dog,
anything smaller than a tennis ball is too small.

Some dogs love squeaky toys, others seem to consider that they have to
immediately kill the source of the squeak. We know of two very small dogs
whose attitude to a squeaky toy is directly opposite to their basic natures. One
of them, a most gentle friendly little creature who never shows any signs of
aggression whatsoever, will immediately destroy a squeaky toy and then lose

all interest. The other, with all the tough characteristics of a terrier, will play for hours making the toy squeak without harming it in any way. The problem is that because the anti-squeak dog is slightly larger, he invariably gains control of the toy and the terrier loses his squeaker!

COLLARS AND LEADS

You have already purchased a good-quality leather collar and lead, but you may find a few other items of equipment will be useful for exercise and training purposes.

THE EXTENSION LEAD: A dog should be kept on a lead all the time when walking in the street. However, when exercising in public places, such as in parks, it may also be necessary that your dog remains on a lead. To enable the dog to get as much free movement as possible while you still retain control, it is advisable to use of one of the long, cord leads which winds around a spring-loaded drum, contained in a plastic handle. The spring-loaded drum means that the lead automatically shortens when the tension is taken off, while any lengthening of the lead can be controlled by a button-operated brake contained in the handle. The automatic shortening of the lead when tension is removed solves the problem of the dog becoming entangled in a long lead, while still allowing a reasonable amount of freedom of movement. Leads of this type can be obtained at any good pet shop, and they come in a variety of sizes to suit small, medium or large dogs.

THE CHOKE CHAIN: For training purposes, the so-called choke or check-chain is popular, especially for use on larger dogs. Despite its name, it does not, if correctly used, choke the dog into submission. It should be used to provide a signal to the dog that if he continues to pull on his lead, this will result in an unpleasant tightening of the collar. When wearing a choke chain, no dog should be allowed to run free without supervision because of the risk of the chain catching in something and strangling the dog. It is important to remember that the check-chain is a training aid, and should not be left on the dog when not in use for this purpose.

THE DOG HARNESS

You can buy a body harness for your dog, and this has a lead attachment between the dog's shoulders. These harnesses are not really suitable for a large dog as they give very little control and allow the dog to tow you along as if he was a carthorse. They are also a bit complicated to put on. However, for a small dog, like a Yorkshire Terrier, who refuses to walk calmly on a lead and reduces himself to a choking wreck by pulling against his collar, the harness can be a useful answer. A harness is also worth considering if your dog has a sensitive throat.

MUZZLES

Most owners would prefer not to use a muzzle on a dog that is a friend and companion. However, there are some circumstances where it may be necessary to use one. The old-fashioned type of muzzle, which consists of an arrangement of straps, has to be very tight to be effective, and a dog can work part of the muzzle between his teeth so that he either bites through it or becomes distressed.

There are two types of muzzle which are suitable. One is the type used by Army and Police dogs consisting of a broad, funnel-shaped band of leather, which fits over the dog's muzzle and is fastened by a strap going back behind the ears. The dog can still breathe easily, but he cannot bite. Unfortunately, this type of muzzle is not suitable for short-nosed breeds such as the Boxer or Bulldog. The alternative is to use a basket-muzzle, made of semi-rigid material, which encloses the head and nose in a basket. This allows the dog to breathe and open his mouth, but he is prevented from biting. Muzzles should not be worn for long periods of time.

THE HEAD COLLAR

If your rescued dog is of a size or nature that suggests that he will be uncooperative when walking on a lead, or at least until you have trained him in the necessary good manners, you may wish to use what is usually described as a "head collar". This is an arrangement of light, nylon straps resembling a loose-fitting muzzle (although it does not really act as one), with the lead attachment ring towards the end of the dog's nose. A pull on the lead turns the dog's head in the direction of the pull; the dog literally has to follow his nose. This device certainly helps to control your dog, but it does little to further his training. It does not replace the basic collar, which the dog should continue to wear even when the head collar is in use.

GROOMING

Whether your dog is long or short-coated, he will need regular grooming sessions. If your dog is long-coated, you will have to groom him more frequently than if he has a short smooth coat. In general, the hair of the dog does not grow continuously as it does in humans. After a time the hair stops growing and eventually falls out. Fresh hair then grows as a replacement. When a dog lives in cold conditions, the hair usually falls out in the spring and in the autumn. This is known as the moult. Modern centrally-heated houses mean that these temperature changes do not occur, and the dog virtually moults continuously. Rather than have this continuous cascade of loose hair on your carpets and chairs, which is then transferred to your clothes and up your nose, you should groom frequently, thus keeping the loose hair on the grooming brush where it can be disposed of.

The exceptions to the rule about moulting are the Poodle, the Yorkshire

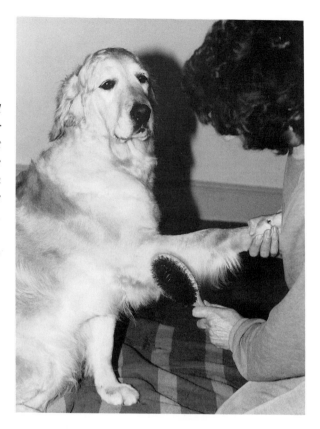

Your dog will need regular grooming. Start by brushing the coat through with a bristle brush.

Steve Nash.

Terrier, and certain related breeds whose coats do not fall out, but continue to grow. With these breeds, not only will you have to groom them to take out the tangles, but they will also need a periodic hair-cut. If you have rescued a Poodle and you want to keep him in a fashionable clip, then you would be advised to employ the services of a professional grooming parlour – at least until you have learnt how to do a reasonable job for yourself. If you attempt to trim your dog's coat, make sure you have someone to hold the dog steady until both you and your dog become used to the procedure. The heavy-coated breeds, like the Old English Sheepdog, look very attractive in full coat provided they are properly groomed. However, for the companion dog it is advisable to keep the coat trimmed fairly short – particularly in the summer months.

If you want to keep your long-coated dog in full coat, make sure you lay aside a period of every day for a grooming session. If you stick to the same time every day, you will not forget – and hopefully, both you and your dog will enjoy these sessions. You only need to spend a few minutes each day brushing out the coat and sorting out any tangles. If you leave it for too long, you will find that much of the coat has tied itself into large knots which defy unravelling, and these will have to be cut out with scissors. It is not unusual to see a long-coated dog who appears to have four ears – the tufts of hair around the ears having matted into a solid lump. No amount of combing will shift these lumps, which soon acquire the toughness and consistency of a thick piece of felt. Cutting the mass away is the only answer, but be careful: it is not always easy to see which is ear and which is coat. For a long-coated dog, you will require a wire brush and a comb. The wire curry combs are useful. Whenever you use any form of wire brush, bear in mind that too vigorous use of it can scratch the dog's skin. Always brush with the lie of the coat, and brush through the coat, layer by layer.

A smooth-coated dog only requires a bristle brush, and what is usually described as a grooming glove. The glove, which may be made out of fabric or rubber, fits over your hand and has usually has two grades of roughness, one on each side. After brushing with the bristle brush, you can complete the job and put a shine on the coat with the glove. Some breeds, the Rottweiler and German Shepherd Dog, for example, have a fairly harsh outer coat and a short soft woolly undercoat. At times, the undercoat may show through the outer coat making the dog look like a badly worn carpet. Using the curry comb, you will find that you can groom out much of the undercoat.

Your dog may not be used to being groomed, and you may need considerable patience to teach him to stand still, or to lie on his side while you are brushing and combing. Talk to your dog reassuringly all the time you are grooming, but be firm if your dog tries to struggle away, so that he understands what is required. Keep the grooming sessions very short to begin with, so that your dog does not come to dread them. In time, when the dog understands that you are not trying to hurt him, he will enjoy getting the extra fuss and attention.

BATHING

You may decide to bath your new dog, and unless you have a very small dog, this could be a traumatic experience for everybody concerned. It is therefore better to wait until your dog has had a chance to settle into his new home. It is highly likely that the dog has never suffered such an indignity before and that he will be extremely unwilling to cooperate. You will probably find that after a major struggle, during which not only your dog but the entire household will be soaked with water, the dog will show his opinion of the proceedings by finding the smelliest patch of filth available and rolling in it!

Bathing your dog removes the natural oils from the coat. A good coat condition comes from a healthy diet and regular grooming. Occasionally, with a very matted long coat, bathing can be a help in disentangling the knots –

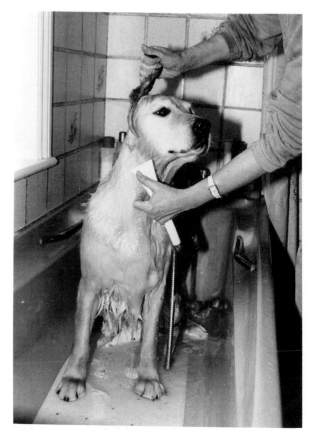

Give your dog a chance to settle into his new home before you attempt to bath him.

Steve Nash.

although it is generally advisable to brush out the coat before bathing. Baths should be kept to the minimum and mainly used as a means of dealing with external parasites, such as fleas and lice, when you will require an insecticidal shampoo, which should be used after seeking the advice of your vet.

If you bath your dog, use an old-fashioned tin bath or children's play pool on the floor of the kitchen or utility room, or if the weather is warm, then you can go outside in the garden. If possible, fix up a shower spray with a length of hose-pipe connected to both the hot and cold taps. A cold-water bath will not only make it difficult to work up a lather, but it will also, understandably, increase the dog's dislike of the whole affair. Dry the dog thoroughly after his bath, and just because your dog is soaking wet, do not shut him out in a cold garden or outside kennel to dry off.

FEET

In theory, claws should not need trimming if a dog has regular exercise on hard ground. In fact, this is only true if the dog has correctly formed feet, so that the ends of the claws are constantly being worn down by being in contact with the ground. The dog may also have dewclaws, which are the claws a little way up the front legs and sometimes also on the rear legs. The dewclaws do not receive any natural wear and can occasionally grow right round and into the leg.

Cutting a dog's nails can be a difficult job. In a large dog, the nail is very tough and you will require a pair of heavy nail-clippers. There is no pain to the dog when you cut through the end of the nail, but it will be painful if you cut too high up into the quick and make it bleed. If you do this the dog will never forgive you, and subsequent chiropody sessions will be difficult. The best approach is a little and often, just removing the tip of the claw each time. This will cause the quick to draw back up the nail, thus allowing you to cut the nail a little shorter each time.

Nail cutting can be a cause of battles between dog and owner, leading to the dog distrusting his owner and resenting all forms of handling. While it may be desirable for your dog to have short nails, it is not worth falling out with the dog, unless the nails are actually causing pain and discomfort. If it is essential that they are cut, then it may be necessary to seek the aid of your vet, who may find that he has to use a general anaesthetic to control the dog before he cuts the nails. As general rule, anaesthetics for a dog should be used as little as possible; you should try to persuade your dog that your gentle use of the clippers is to his advantage.

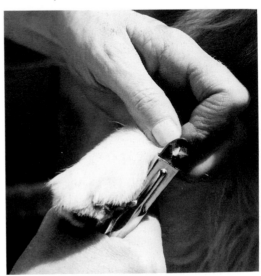

Nail-clippers can be used to keep your dog's nails in trim, but you must make sure you have your dog's trust before attempting this task.

Steve Nash.

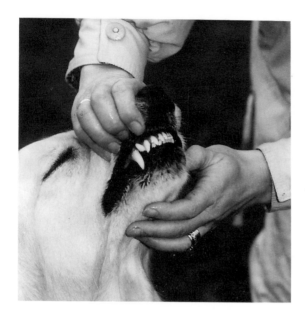

*Regular brushing
with a toothbrush
and water, or using
special dog tooth-
paste, will help to
keep your dog's teeth
free from tartar.*

Steve Nash.

TEETH

Chewing something hard like a bone or a biscuit will help to keep teeth free
from tartar, although it can still build up as the dog grows older. Very
occasionally, you will find that an older dog will have trouble with a bad tooth,
but it is rare for the dog to show signs of painful toothache. If it does, then ask
your vet to deal with it. You can try regular brushing with a toothbrush and
water, and there is even a special toothpaste available for dogs. However, your
dog will need to be a fairly placid individual, or well-trained, to submit to
having his teeth cleaned on a regular basis. If your dog does have to have a
general anaesthetic for any reason, it is worthwhile asking your vet to scale the
teeth at the same time.

EARS

You should check your dog's ears at regular intervals. Long-coated dogs can
grow an excessive amount of hair in the ears. This prevents the air getting into
the ear and traps dust, dirt and wax, causing inflammation and infection. Trim
away any excess hair that you can from the ear canal, and use a cotton bud
moistened with liquid paraffin to remove wax. Be careful not to probe too
deeply into the ear, as you could easily do more harm than good. If the ear is
swollen or reddened, or if it has an unpleasant smell, then consult your vet, who
will probably give you some type of ear-drop to cure the infection.

Check your dog's ears at regular intervals to ensure they are clean. If you need to clean them, do not probe too deeply.

Steve Nash.

CLEANING UP AFTER YOUR DOG

With more and more dogs living in an urban environment you owe it to your dog, the community in general, and also to the law, to ensure that your dog does not contribute to the fouling of public places. Even the most ardent dog lover must admit that public pavements, the neighbour's front lawn, children's playgrounds and sports fields are not suitable places for your dog to deposit its excrement. Equally, your dog has to go somewhere. If you have a garden of your own, then this is the most suitable place. If you have a small kennel and run in the garden with a concrete base, then we suggest that when the dog is first let out in the morning, after meals, and last thing at night, let the dog go in the run where it is easy for you to clear up. The only problem you may have is that some bitches refuse to spend a penny anywhere unless the surface is grass.

If you cannot use a run, then you will have to suffer the brown patches on your lawn. Either way you will have to dispose of the end product. One of the most effective answers is the dog loo. This is a plastic-lidded container about the size of a normal two-gallon bucket. It is sunk in the ground, with the lid level with the top of the soil. All you have to do is shovel everything up and drop it in. It comes complete with a supply of chemicals, which reduces the dog droppings to liquid, which then drains away harmlessly into the ground. At the same time, the chemicals prevent any unpleasant odours. Any caravan enthusiast will be aware of the principles of the system.

There are still areas where it is possible for your dog to run free and allow natural processes to dispose of the result. Such areas are becoming more and more scarce, and even in such areas you should 'pick up' after your dog. When taking your dog out in public, we suggest that you carry a supply of small plastic bags – many pet shops sell bags designed for the purpose. Put the bag on like a glove, pick up the droppings, and then turn the bag inside out. You can also use the bags with a "pooper scooper" which aids picking up. The result is a nice hygienic package which can be dropped into the special receptacle which many park authorities now provide, or otherwise disposed of.

CAR TRAVEL

Like humans, some dogs suffer from car-sickness while others have no problems. Again, like humans, most dogs grow out of being car-sick, but it is obviously preferable if you do not allow the condition to occur. Start off by letting your dog get used to the car when it is stationary. When the dog has learnt to settle, go on a short journey and distract the dog by talking to him and reassuring him. You can even sing, in the hope that the dog will become so intrigued by the noise that he will forget about being sick.

Watch for the first signs of car-sickness, which are drooling and swallowing, and act immediately to distract your dog. If possible, do not feed your dog before a trip in the car, and confine yourself to short trips, always ending up with a walk or a play. If car-sickness persists, your vet can prescribe drugs that may prevent the condition, and there are also effective homeopathic remedies available.

If you need to leave your dog in the car in warm weather, make sure it is parked in the shade with adequate ventilation. In this situation, you will have a problem with the conflicting needs of security and fresh air. On a hot day with the car parked in the sun it is quite inadequate to leave just a couple of inches of open window, and dogs should never be left alone in these circumstances.

One answer is to take Granny along with her knitting or a good book, and leave her in charge of both the car and the dog. The best answer, if your car is either an estate or hatch back, is to buy one of the fitted cages made to measure for your car. These cages fill the whole of the rear of the car and can be kept in position with a chain and padlock. A second padlock can be fitted to the cage door. Using such a cage you can lock the car doors while leaving the tail gate in the up position. The dog can see out and has plenty of fresh air while the interior of the car remains secure. It is important to make sure that the car is always parked in the shade. Always take a plastic bottle of water and a dish when you go out for the day in the car with your dog.

EXERCISE

Dogs are as adaptable over exercise as they are with other aspects of their lifestyle. Within reason, they can take it or leave it. They are also creatures of habit, and if you make a practice of "taking the dog for a walk" at five minutes to opening time at your local pub (provided that you can find one that admits dogs), then the dog will come to expect it. The bigger the dog, the more exercise he will need. A tiny toy dog will probably get most of what he needs trotting around the house and garden, and a walk around the park will be enjoyed as a change of scene and a fresh set of smells, rather than as an opportunity to stretch his legs.

Exercise is a means of stimulating your dog, and the time you spend out together will help in forming a good relationship. Your dog may not need to go for a long gallop every day, but if the outing is always interesting – taking different routes, and playing games at different parts of the walk – your dog's mind will be exercised as well as his body. If you have an intelligent dog, particularly if you have a breed with a strong working background, such as a Border Collie/Working Sheepdog, this form of mental stimulation is essential. A bored dog soon becomes a destructive or delinquent dog, and you must guard against this happening.

Opportunities for a dog to run free outside your own garden are becoming less and less common. It may be necessary for you to travel some distance in order to find areas where it is possible to let your dog off the lead, and even then you can have problems with keeping away from farm livestock and crops. Many beaches now ban dogs during the summer months, and so a visit to the seaside with the opportunity for your dog to chase a ball into the surf, is not always an option. However, if you use a little ingenuity, and allow your dog to run after a ball, or meet up with a friend who has a dog that will play nicely with yours, you can give sufficient exercise in a fairly limited space.

You may be a family that likes to take long country rambles. If so, by all means take the dog with you, provided that he is a fairly large and fit dog who is able to cover the distance. Remember that if a dog is running backwards and forwards during the walk, he will probably cover twice as much ground as you do. A Toy dog will be game enough to start with, but you might have to carry him if he gets too tired. Remember that exercise is related to age as well as size. If your rescued dog is in middle or advancing age, he will not need as much exercise as a youngster. Commonsense will tell you what is the right amount of exercise to give to your dog.

If you have children, it is sensible to encourage them to play a part in exercising the dog. However, children should never be allowed to take a large and powerful dog out in a public place without adult supervision, unless parents are quite certain that they are capable of physically controlling the dog. Your dog may be well-behaved and obedient, but you could meet another dog, possibly without his owner, who will provoke an argument – and your dog could well respond.

Your dog will grow older. He will become stiff in the joints and will slow down, so that what used to be a pleasant stroll becomes hard work for him. Too often you see the owner striding out and the dog dragging behind. The dog, being a courageous creature, will do his best to keep up – but the walk is no longer a pleasure. So be sympathetic to the changing needs of your dog. Go for shorter walks, but introduce more variety to keep your old friend happy and stimulated.

NEUTERING

There is one decision that you may have to make – although it may have already been made for you. If you are rehoming a bitch, should she be neutered?

Many of the welfare bodies have a policy of neutering bitches before they go to their new owners, or alternatively, asking the new owner to have the operation carried out. While you may be unhappy about this policy, a little thought will show you that it is not unreasonable. Many of the dogs that the rescue organisations handle are the result of accidental matings and unwanted litters. It is, therefore, sensible that the organisations should endeavour to reduce the problem, rather than be instrumental in the production of even more puppies, which may, in turn, become in need of rescue. Neutering also offers advantages to the new owner, and as the owner of a rescued dog, you are hardly likely to wish to make money from your kindness by attempting to make a profit by producing litters of puppies.

THE IN-SEASON BITCH

If your rescued bitch has not been neutered when you receive her, then you should consider whether it is desirable to have her neutered. To make this decision you need to understand the problem. A bitch can only be mated when she is in season or "on heat". She will probably come on heat roughly every six months, but it may be more, or less, frequent. The first sign that she is coming on heat is usually that the vulva swells and shows a slight bloody discharge. This will go on for about nine or ten days. The discharge will then cease, and the bitch will probably allow a male to mate her at about the twelfth day after the commencement of her heat. She may continue to stand for mating for about a further nine days. Nature being what it is, these timings are by no means exact, and it is not uncommon for bitches to be successfully mated much earlier in their heats or very much later – sometimes as much as twenty-three days from the commencement of the heat. You must therefore appreciate that if your bitch is not neutered, there is a risk that she will succeed in getting herself mated, and this risk will occur probably twice a year.

Do not get tempted by the idea that it will be fun to have a litter of puppies, as well as being a useful biology lesson for the children. You will have plenty of time to regret your decision when you have up to a dozen rumbustious ten-week-old youngsters wrecking your house, costing a fortune to feed, and all those friends and neighbours who assured you that they would love a puppy, now making their excuses. This is the moment when you are at grave risk of adding to the problem of too many dogs needing to be rescued. So please do not be tempted.

To sum up the problem. If your bitch is not neutered, then for two or three times a year you are going to have to keep her safe from the attention of amorous males. This is not as easy as it sounds. When the bitch is ready, she may not be the shy little girl that she normally is. She may be only too ready to escape from purdah and cooperate in getting herself mated – we once had a tiny Chihuahua who would stand on the third step of the stairs, in the hope of solving the problems involved with mating to our large Boxer dog! If you take your in-season bitch for a walk, you will find that you are leading a mob of the local canine street-corner boys, who will follow you home and camp out on your doorstep. The mating that you do not want can happen very quickly. Many unwanted litters are excused by the owners on the grounds that they "only turned their back for a moment".

HORMONE THERAPY
Apart from keeping your bitch shut in, there are two possible ways of preventing your bitch from becoming pregnant. The first is by the use of hormones. This method can produce a temporary solution in that it will prevent pregnancy during a particular heat. However, it can have the effect of merely postponing the season, which recurs again at less than the normal interval. There is also the risk that you will miss the signs of the bitch coming in heat, and so the use of the hormones will be too late. If you decide to attempt this method of contraception for your bitch, you should discuss the matter very thoroughly with your vet.

SPAYING
The second method of preventing pregnancy is by the surgical removal of the ovaries and uterus, known as spaying. This operation is, of course, permanent and irreversible. Most modern veterinary opinion is that this can be done at an early age, probably after the first season, which is usually at about nine months of age. It is sometimes carried out at an even younger age, before the first season. We have never seen any indication that spaying will have an adverse effect on a bitch's temperament. In fact, many of the most gentle and sweet-natured bitches that we have known have been spayed. A bitch's maternal instincts only apply when she has a young litter to nurse. Spaying does not mean that your bitch will go through life regretting that she is not a mother.

However, the operation may lead to obesity, and it may be necessary to control the amount of food that she is given, and possibly to increase her exercise. With regard to rescued bitches, there is no doubt that spaying is a useful and sensible practice with virtually no disadvantages. The operation is simple and safe, and while you may feel that it is wrong to meddle with nature, it is far kinder to the bitch to have her spayed than to allow her to have a succession of unwanted litters.

CASTRATION

Neutering of male dogs by castration is sometimes used to curb unwanted sexual activity and also to prevent aggression against other male dogs. For example, all males working as Guide Dogs for the Blind are castrated because it is obviously undesirable to have such a dog getting into fights, or dragging his owner down the street in pursuit of an in-season bitch. However, castration is not necessarily the solution with a dog who is unreliable with children, destructive, or aggressive towards humans, although it may help.

REGISTRATION AND INSURANCE

In the past, the Dog Licence offered no benefits to the dog owner, and at the time dog licensing was dropped, it cost more to collect than it brought the Government in revenue.The so far unsuccessful attempts to reintroduce such a licence would, in the form that has been suggested, have merely imposed a tax on dogs, without benefit to either dogs or their owners. The only form of registration which would benefit the dog owner is one by which, if the dog went missing, it could be identified and traced back to the owner through a central and national register. Government has so far shown no inclination to introduce such a scheme. However, there are a number of registers run by private organisations which offer means of identification linked to a central record which enables the owner of a lost dog to be traced and reunited with their pet. The disadvantage of such schemes is that the police or other authority holding the stray dog has no means of knowing which, if any, scheme it is registered with. Registration does offer you some hope of recovering your lost dog, and it follows that the greatest chance of success is with the scheme that has the greatest coverage and gives the maximum publicity to its service.

The scheme which appears to best fit these criteria is the one operated by the National Pet Register in conjunction with the Wood Green Animal Shelters at Royston in Hertfordshire. For a very small sum, they offer a lifelong registration for your dog, the necessary identification disc, and a one-year third party insurance cover. They also provide facilities for you to notify them when you are away on holiday, and if the dog is lost during this period, they provide care of the dog until you can be contacted. The third party insurance cover is renewable annually. While you may consider that insurance for the death of your dog or for veterinary treatment is rather expensive, third party insurance covering you against an accident caused by your dog, or by your dog biting someone is something every dog owner should have.

The law requires that your dog should wear some form of identification on his collar, giving your name and address. This regulation is being strictly enforced nowadays, and if your dog gets out on to the street without a collar and identification, then you run a real risk of the dog being picked up by a dog warden and taken to a holding kennels. It will cost you money to retrieve your dog – assuming you can find out where he has been taken. (You should always ring the local authority and the police if you have lost your dog.) Although there are various means of identification on the market, there is no better answer than the old-fashioned engraved metal disc or tag, securely fastened to the collar with a split ring. The small metal barrel, consisting of two halves screwed together, containing a slip of paper with all your details, is not a good alternative. Rescue kennels are full of dogs with half the barrel hanging from their collars and the vital piece of paper missing.

Apart from the engraved disc on the collar, there are other forms of identification for your dog. These include tattooing, an implanted transponder which can be read with a hand-held reader (rather like the system used at many supermarket checkouts), and freeze marking. All these methods are virtually impossible to erase and give a permanent means of identification, unlike the disc which can be removed.

If you consider that one of the permanent identification systems is desirable, then the implanted transponder is not as fearsome as it sounds. A minute micro-chip is injected under the skin. Irrespective of the size or type of dog, it is always placed in the back of the neck so that the person using the reader knows where to look. The chip is totally inert so that there is no question of your dog walking around with a science fiction gadget stuck in his neck. In fact, it offers much less intrusion than, for example, a metal pin used by a vet to repair a fracture. The implantation is virtually painless – probably no more than the dog suffers when he gets his annual booster injections – and it is sealed in the same way as a human pacemaker, so that there can be no possibility of any adverse effect.

It was claimed at one time that the chip could migrate around the dog's body, but improvements in the method of injection have solved this problem. Finally, the reading head is able to decode any one of the nine different micro-chips that are in use. Because most of us are sentimental about our dogs, we are unhappy about anything which would appear to interfere with nature. In spite of these perfectly understandable objections, if you have a need for positive and permanent identification, the micro-chip is almost certainly the answer.

Another very useful service provided by the Wood Green Animal Shelter is the Pet Alert Card. All of us worry about what might happen to our dogs if we were unable to look after them as a result of an accident or unexpected illness. The Pet Alert Card comes in two sizes. One is suitable to carry in your pocket, and the other to display in your house or car. Their purpose is to call the attention of any stranger dealing with the situation to the existence of your dogs, and to instruct them as to who to contact to look after them.

Chapter Four
FEEDING AND DIET

THE RIGHT START

Before going into rescue kennels, your dog may have been fed on a low-quality diet. It is important to avoid the temptation of over-compensating by feeding large amounts of rich food. This will be disastrous for your dog's digestive system. To begin with, you should follow the diet used at the rescue kennels, and then introduce any changes gradually.

It is probable that your whole family will want to be present at the first meal that your dog is given in his new home. Everyone will want to see the dog start on his new life, and will expect him to eat his carefully prepared dinner with enthusiasm. However, if your dog has been neglected by his previous owner it is likely that it will have learned to scavenge for his food, and he may become frightened, secretive and guilty when expected to "eat in public". If this happens, leave the dog alone with his meal, and, with luck, when you come back a few minutes later the dog will have cleared his dish.

It is not generally advisable to leave a dish of uneaten food down overnight, but this may be an occasion when you should do so. Under cover of darkness, the dog will feel it is safe to eat. If the dog has not eaten by the next morning, remove the food and try tempting him with something else. You cannot sit there like an old-fashioned parent saying: "You will stay there until you have eaten your dinner." Some dogs would rather starve.

If, in the past, your dog has been chased out of the kitchen and scolded for eating from the dinner plates, then you may find that he is unwilling to eat from a dish. Try throwing the food on the floor or even outside in the garden. Some dogs have odd phobias about where they eat. We even came across one dog who would only eat crouched under the front seat of the family car. It may very well be that food has been something that has had to be stolen and eaten in secret. It doesn't really matter where your dog eats, as long as he eats somewhere. Try feeding him under the bed or behind the dustbin. All this might sound messy and slightly absurd, but you do not know what has happened to the dog during his earlier life, and at this stage the important thing is to get the dog eating. When your dog gains confidence and starts to trust you, it will not be long before he adopts a more conventional feeding pattern.

If your rescued dog is a puppy, you must feed good-quality food, spread over three or four meals a day.

FEEDING A PUPPY

If your rescued dog is a young puppy – under six months of age – you will need to feed more concentrated food than you would for an adult. A puppy needs large quantities of food in relation to his body weight, but it has a stomach of smaller capacity. The dry, complete foods, which you can feed to adults, can be difficult to digest for young puppies. However, if you feed a diet which is especially designed for puppies, it is advisable to soak the food before feeding.

A puppy should have its total daily food allocation spread over three or four meals per day. Gradually, the food intake can be reduced to two or three meals per day until at about a year to eighteen months the dog goes on to an adult routine. Reducing the frequency of meals does not mean cutting down the quantity of food. On the contrary, the total daily amount must be increased as the dog grows.

FEEDING THE ADULT DOG

Apart from puppies and young adults up to about eighteen months of age, whose food intake should be spread over several meals, one main meal per day should be adequate for an adult dog. When you feed your dog is a matter of personal convenience, but whatever time of day you select for the main meal, it should be adhered to. The dog's tummy clock will soon settle into a routine and you will have a very puzzled and unhappy dog if dinner is at 10 o'clock in the morning one day and 10 o'clock in the evening the next. However, it will not be the end of its world if you are occasionally half an hour late or early to suit your convenience. We like to feed the main meal during the early evening so that the dog has a full stomach during the night, helping him to sleep and giving him time to digest his food in peace. The dog will probably wake up hungry, so you can give a breakfast of a handful of dry biscuits. Your dog may enjoy a saucer of tea, given at the same time.

FOOD QUANTITIES

Because your rescued dog may vary in size from a tiny Yorkshire Terrier to something the size of a Great Dane, it is impossible to lay down precise quantities of food required each day. If you are using one of the manufactured foods, there will almost certainly be instructions on the package as to the correct quantities for a given weight of dog. These days, such weights will probably be given in kilos, and you will need to know what your dog weighs. Provided that the dog is not too big, you can solve this by taking the dog in your arms and standing on the bathroom scales. You will need an assistant to read the scales as it is usually impossible to see down past the dog to read your combined weights. You then weigh yourself without the dog, take your weight from the total, and you have the dog's weight.

It will not be good for your dog's health if you attribute to him more than his fair share of your combined weights and over-feed him as a result. If you are using a proprietary food as a complete diet you can safely feed to their instructions. If, however, you are using such foods as a part of your mixture, then you will need to reduce the laid down quantity of each proprietary food. Achieving the correct amount of food for a given dog must inevitably be a matter of judgement. Some dogs, like some humans, will put on weight on very little food, others will eat very large meals and still remain slim.

The aim should be to give your dog as much food as he will eat while maintaining his reasonably slim figure. If your dog shows signs of becoming overweight then reduce the quantity, or possibly cut down the amount of fattening foods. If you think that your dog is looking thin, then increase the size of his helpings. Dogs that are taking a lot of exercise will usually require more food than the 'couch potatoes' who are content to lie around the house for most of the day.

A dog can be given titbits as a treat or as a reward, but these should be very tiny and not in sufficient amounts to have a major effect on the diet. There is no point in designing a balanced diet for the given meal, and then allowing the dog unlimited access to the biscuit box. We recall one loving owner who proudly produced the eighteen-month-old Rottweiler which we had sold her as a puppy. To our horror, the dog was so fat that he could hardly walk. The owner assured us that she had stuck rigidly to the diet sheet that we had given her. Further questioning revealed that although the dog's meals were in accordance with our diet sheet, the dog had constant access to a washing-up bowl which was kept full of dog biscuits – just in case he felt peckish between meals!

CHOOSING YOUR DOG'S DIET

Providing food for pets is a multi-million pound business. The sales of dog and cat foods in Britain in 1992 exceeded £1billion, and the industry spent £37 million promoting its products. An enormous choice of food is offered, not only of ingredients but of special diets, ranging from gourmet meals to between-meal snacks and titbits. The range includes special high-calorie foods for working dogs, low-calorie foods for obese dogs, and special diets for nursing bitches. There are foods designed for puppies, and for canine old-age pensioners. There are vegetarian diets for dogs who require such diets, or whose owners are vegetarians and want their dog to be the same. Dog food comes in tins, frozen, dried, vacuum-packed or in the form of biscuits, meal or pellets.

There is no doubt that an enormous amount of work and research goes into producing a safe, healthy product, although we suspect that much of the packaging and the contents are primarily intended to appeal to the human owner rather than the dog. However, the industry has been very successful in taking waste human food products which are unsuitable for, or unattractive to humans, and processing them in such a way as to make them look attractive to the human purchasers. The dog would probably have eaten the food in its original form – but the owner would not have bought it! It has been said that the industry is "all about turning rubbish into a usable product without creating health hazards". Certainly, the multitude of health regulations means that you will have the greatest difficulty in obtaining fresh food for your dog, unless you buy food intended for human consumption. The days when you could buy large lumps of pet-quality meat or fresh tripe are sadly gone.

What you actually feed your dog must depend on a number of factors. A very small dog eating tiny quantities can be fed on human-quality foods without the cost being prohibitive. We know of two very small dogs whose weekly diet consists of two boiled chickens, a small amount of good-quality biscuit, a few between-meals treats, and the odd titbit from their owner's plate. Both of them are very fit, their motions are excellent, and they are not overweight. The total cost for the two of them is certainly no more than the price of three packets of cigarettes per week, and – in their owner's opinion – far better value. However, cost would become a major factor in the feeding of a large dog using human-quality food, and with the many options available, there is no necessity to do this.

A BALANCED DIET

Your dog requires a balanced diet, meaning that the diet should contain the necessary proteins, fats, carbohydrates, vitamins and minerals. What constitutes a balanced diet can be the subject of some debate. Although the dog is technically carnivorous, it is better described as omnivorous. A dog is able to survive on either an animal diet or a vegetable diet. In the wild state, the dog ate other animals, including the stomach contents which were probably vegetable, and added roots, fruit etc. to achieve a balance. However, the dog has been with man a very long time, and in the same way that it has modified its mental attitude, it has also adapted its digestion. For some groups of dogs the satisfactory diet for generations has been what it was able to get. Extreme examples are the Border Collie, traditionally fed on oatmeal, and the Husky fed on seal meat, which is two-thirds fat. Both groups work extremely hard in an adverse environment, and yet they remain fit and healthy. Through the centuries the domestic dog has become extremely flexible in its dietary needs. Humans also require a balanced diet. However, few of us spend long hours calculating our precise needs for every meal. Instead, we eat a varied diet and our bodies sort out what we need and reject the rest. Within reasonable limits the dog will do the same. The pet food manufacturers will tell you that their complete foods or, in some cases, a combination of their products provide a balanced diet. You can therefore solve your problem by browsing along the supermarket shelves, reading the labels, and allowing your own tastes and purse-size to govern your decision. If you decide to feed your dog solely with the products of the pet food industry, then it is almost certain that your dog will have a healthy diet and you will avoid the need to think about the subject. However, with the very wide choice of types of food available on the market you still need to have some knowledge before making your choice.

PROPRIETARY DOG FOODS
Basically, proprietary dog foods come either in tins or some other air-tight container, or as dry food in the form of extruded pellets or a mixture of various dried vegetable and cereal products, usually fortified with some form of dried meat pellet. In general, you have two choices. Firstly, "complete diets" which contain everything that your dog will need, usually in a dry form either as pellets or meal. Secondly, you can use some form of tinned or vacuum-packed tinned "meat", which may or may not be all meat – although it probably looks like it – used in conjunction with a "mixer" pellet sold separately.

TINNED FOOD: The tinned and vacuum-packed products vary enormously in price and presentation. Some of them may prove to be too rich for your dog, and certainly, in our experience, they can act as an unrequired laxative if the dog is not used to them. The canine equivalents of caviare and steak, pleasant as they may be, are by no means necessary as a full-time diet. At the bottom of the price range, the product appears to consist largely of cereal and fish, which can be used together with a general-purpose biscuit as a basic maintenance diet.

COMPLETE DIETS: The top end of the range of the dry "all-in-one" complete diets are usually in pellet or kibbled form. They are very carefully formulated, and while they are expensive, they do provide an excellent diet. Some of the best use chicken as a major part of the contents, and the manufacturers point out that they exclude the use of the head, feet, feathers and bones. However, we have reservations about the source of some of the contents used by some manufacturers. For example, protein can be animal, vegetable, or even manufactured from chemicals such as oil. Some of the all-in-one dry foods tend to be bulky, in that the dog requires a large quantity to satisfy its nutritional needs. This is a factor that is worth considering, as you will almost certainly have to clear up the resulting motions.

BISCUIT MEAL: Apart from the all-in-one foods and the complementary meat and mixer foods, there is a wide range of biscuits and meals available on the market. These are intended to be used in conjunction with some form of protein such as meat, either tinned, frozen or fresh. The best of the biscuits are wholemeal, and some include added vitamins and calcium. The manufacturers of many of the dry complete diets suggest that you feed their product in its dry state. Apart from the fact that it looks extremely boring as a diet, we have always worried about the possibility of the dry food expanding in the dog's stomach, resulting in the very dangerous condition known as "bloat". For this reason – and because it would appear to make the diet more palatable – we have always soaked both biscuits and complete diets with either gravy or hot water for about an hour before feeding.

HOUSEHOLD SCRAPS: We have covered the question of feeding manufactured food at considerable length. There is no doubt that it is the simplest and most convenient method of giving your dog a satisfactory diet. However, many dogs are still fed on household scraps, with or without the addition of commercial pet foods, and in the rest of Europe the percentage of dogs fed in this way is far higher. There is no reason why you should not use leftover human food for your dog, provided that you understand the principles involved. We would suggest that approximately twenty per cent of your dog's diet can be made up from what you and your family leave on your plates, the rest of the diet being made up of your choice of manufactured dog foods.

NUTRITIONAL VALUES
If you are using leftovers as part of your dog's diet, it is important to understand the value and effect of feeding some of the more common foods likely to be available in the average household.

MEAT: Dogs like meat, and it is a good source of protein. It is not, however, sufficient as a complete diet. It needs to be fed in conjunction with other food such as biscuits or one of the complete foods, which will provide the extra calcium and vitamins that are needed. It should not form more than twenty-five per cent of the total diet. If you are certain that the meat is fresh and healthy it may be fed raw, but you are probably safer to boil it, using the gravy to soak the accompanying biscuit.

LIVER: Again, a good source of protein and vitamins. It should only be fed occasionally and not to excess. Liver should always be cooked. Uncooked liver is unpalatable to most dogs, and it is also extremely laxative.

EGGS: A good source of protein and vitamins. If fed raw, only the yolks should be used as the raw whites have the effect of destroying some vitamins. The best method is to hard-boil or scramble the whole egg and add it to whatever else the dog is having for dinner that day. Eggs can also play a part in the treatment of diarrhoea.

BONES: Chewing on a large bone can help to maintain healthy gums and remove plaque and tartar from the teeth. However, constant chewing on hard bones can wear down and break the dog's teeth, giving problems in old age. Although almost traditional, bones are by no means essential to the modern dog. A handful of hard biscuits a day will have the same cleansing effect on tartar and plaque.

You should only give large uncooked bones; they should not be small or likely to splinter. Dogs may be possessive over bones, and they can be a cause of a dog snapping if he thinks that you or a child are about to remove his treasure. One bone a week is quite sufficient, and after a good chew for an hour or so, the bone should be removed to avoid your dog building up a collection – usually stored under the cushions of your best sofa, to the discomfort of your visitors.

MILK: This contains most nutrients. It is, after all, a complete food. Some adult dogs cannot digest milk, and given in large quantities it can be a cause of diarrhoea. However, most dogs can digest small quantities of milk, and there is no reason why you should not add the last drop in the milk bottle to their diet. Milk cooked as a rice pudding or custard is usually much more digestible. If your dog is able to take milk in large quantities and you have a cheap source of supply, then by all means use it. We know of one very successful breeder of one of the giant breeds who gave a daily bucketful from her Jersey cows, and her dogs were always in excellent condition.

VEGETABLES: Green vegetables, such as cabbage, do not have a great feeding value for the dog, although they do contain some useful vitamins. If you have a small amount of cooked cabbage left over, it is worth adding to the dog bowl rather than throwing it away. Potatoes and carrots, if cooked, are quite acceptable – but do not try and save money by using potatoes as a major part of the diet. Carrot can also be given raw if a small amount is grated over the food.

BREAD: Wholemeal bread is preferable to white because it contains more fibre. Soaked in gravy, it is a satisfactory, occasional replacement for all or part of the biscuit part of the diet.

CHEESE: This is a good source of calcium and phosphorus. Any leftovers, including the rind, can be put in the dog's bowl.

RICE: Plain boiled rice is good, and it is especially useful for dogs with stomach disorders. (We do not recommend that you include the remainder of your Chinese takeaway!)

BISCUITS: This refers to the conventional dog biscuits which come in a variety of sizes from about an inch-square to giant doorsteps that can only be broken with a hammer. They are useful as a small snack meal, providing roughage and energy. Chewing hard biscuits can assist keeping your dog's teeth clean and will also help to keep him amused. Some of them come in a variety of colours, each containing a different mineral. Black biscuits contain charcoal as an aid to digestion, and although the manufacturers are too polite to mention it, these can also reduce flatulence.

WATER: Lack of water can kill a dog by dehydration far quicker than lack of food. Your dog should have free access to a bowl of clean, cool water at all times. Even though there is still water in its bowl, it should be replaced frequently. How would you like your pint of beer to be covered with a thin film of dust, plus a garnish of a couple of dead moths? You should form an estimate of the normal amount of water that your dog drinks, making allowance for an increase during hot weather or after exercise. The type of diet will affect the water intake. Tinned dog food may contain as much as eighty per cent water, while dry food may be as low as ten per cent. It follows that if you use one of the all-in-one diets and feed it dry, then your dog will require more water than if fed on tinned food. Excessive drinking for no obvious cause can be a sign of illness, and if it persists you should consult your vet.

SUPPLEMENTS

Your pet shop will probably stock a number of supplements that you can add to your dog's diet. These should be used with care. Some years ago, it became fashionable to add extra vitamins, calcium etc., to a dog's diet. It was believed that a dog would use what it required and excrete the rest. As a result, dogs were developing various conditions such as bone malformation, which were eventually traced to the excessive use of vitamins and other supplements. Owners trying to do their best for their dogs were, in fact, doing them severe harm. The situation became even more complicated when owners started to add proprietary products or cod-liver oil – and sometimes both – to complete diets, which already contained the correct balance of supplements.

Supplements can have a place in a diet which is deficient in minerals or vitamins, provided they are used in accordance with the instructions of the manufacturer. If you are using one of the good-quality complete diets then it is unlikely that you will need to add supplements. If you do use supplements, you should be aware that both proprietary supplements and also cod-liver oil can be toxic if used to excess. Yeast tablets which are a source of vitamin B have no known ill effects, and if used should be given as for humans, but scaled down by weight. Some people swear by garlic added to the diet, although others claim it is of no value. It is usually given in the form of tablets, and it would appear to act as a internal cleansing agent. Many people believe that it is an aid to disease prevention – certainly, we have never found its use to be harmful.

Obviously, if your dog develops a condition which your vet diagnoses as being due to some sort of diet deficiency then you will modify the diet, or add a supplement under expert guidance. Apart from such reasons, your dog is unlikely to need any additive, provided that you either use a complete food as the sole diet or feed a reasonably varied mixture of foods.

MEALS

Assuming that you decide that you will make use of household scraps, we suggest that the bulk of the meal is made up of one of the good-quality, dry, all-in-one foods and a good-quality wholemeal biscuit in the proportions of half and half. This should be soaked with either hot water or gravy. Use just enough liquid to moisten and soften the mixture. Do not use so much liquid that the whole thing becomes a sort of sloppy porridge. To this, you should add a small helping of one of the tinned dog foods and whatever scraps the family have left that day.

Unlike humans, dogs are not nauseated by outlandish combinations of flavour and will not be put off if you add the oil from a tin of sardines to a dish which already contains meat, cabbage, cheese, bacon rind, and half a hard-boiled egg.

SPECIAL DIETS: Hopefully your dog will not need any form of special diet, at least until he is getting old. However, it is possible that diet may need special consideration either because of some permanent condition or as a measure to cure a temporary condition. You will need the advice of your vet if this is the case. For example, dogs suffering from diabetes need a diet high in energy and carbohydrates, while a dog suffering from nephritis (inflammation of the kidneys) needs a low protein diet of high quality. Occasionally a dog will be unable to digest meat, and if this is so there are a number of proprietary vegetarian diets available.

PROBLEM FEEDERS

You may have the problem of a dog who is a finicky feeder. This is usually a temporary condition brought on by stress or indigestion. Usually, it is a question of getting the dog to start eating again by using some small titbit, such as cooked liver, cheese or chicken, after which the stomach takes over and the dog will eat normally. Such a dog can sometimes be tempted by highly-spiced or flavoured foods such as a few pieces of kipper, with the bones removed, or a couple of sardines. Commercial cat foods, which are more highly flavoured than dog foods, may also be effective.

Depending on what you are feeding your dog, an old dog person's trick is to chew a small amount of the food yourself and then give it to the dog. This is a reversion to puppyhood when the bitch weaned her puppies by regurgitating her own food for them. There is no need for you to take a large mouthful of the sort of meals we have been describing in this section. A spoonful of your own food or a piece of bread and butter will be just as successful.

It is possible that a dog who has lived with his owner for a number of years before needing to be rehomed will have never seen or tasted proprietary dog food. The dog may have lived his entire life on scraps and titbits from his owner's plate, probably washed down with a saucer of tea. Such a dog will need to be tempted with similar meals. We have found that human digestive biscuits, perhaps accompanied by something like a small helping of minced chicken, will often prove attractive.

A temporary failure to eat is probably nothing to worry about. It can happen when a dog is exhausted by vigorous exercise, or if he is distracted by some other factor such as a bitch in season. However, persistent refusal of food can be a sign of serious illness, and your vet should be consulted if this continues for more than about thirty-six hours.

Some dogs may be eating well, but remain thin. This is not unusual in an adolescent dog, especially if the dog is active. In fact, it is better that a growing dog should be fairly lean rather than carry excess fat. Excessive thinness coupled with a large appetite can be a sign of a heavy infestation of worms, or some disease. In these circumstances you should consult your vet. There are a number of diets on the market which can help you to put weight on your dog.

Indigestion is often indicated by a "rumbling tummy". The stomach rumbles are often quite loud and can be heard across the room, or you may hear them by putting your ear close to the dog's stomach. When this happens, your dog may show an almost uncontrollable desire to eat grass. Do not worry. Your dog has not turned into a sheep, neither, as some people will tell you, is he searching for some vital mineral lacking from his diet. Having grazed, the dog will probably come indoors and vomit the grass covered in frothy saliva all over your carpet. A dog uses grass to relieve an excess of digestive juices which have accumulated in an empty stomach.

We have found that children's "gripe water" or some other antacid remedy, given in a dosage which would correspond to the amount given to a child of the same weight, is the easy answer. Use a spoon and pour it into the corner of the dog's mouth. If you are interested in using homoeopathic remedies, then *nux vom* or *arsen alb*, given in the recommended manner and dosage, are very effective especially for small dogs. Do not allow your dog to eat grass from roadside verges or other areas which may have been treated with poisonous pesticides.

You may find that your dog regurgitates his food in the form of a long sausage of chewed food, brought up from the gullet rather than the stomach. If this happens it will be within minutes of having eaten. Your understandable reaction will be to scold the dog, rush for a cleaning cloth and, if you are kind-hearted, give the dog some fresh food. In fact, you should do none of these things. Leave the food where it is, say nothing to the dog and in a moment the dog will probably eat the food and this time it will stay down. This action is quite common and can be considered normal in some dogs. It is usually caused by the dog bolting his food too quickly. Grumbling at the dog will make him become frightened at feeding time and probably spoil his appetite. If this type of vomiting happens too frequently, then feed the dog outside or on a sheet of newspaper. If in doubt, consult your vet.

Chapter Five

TRAINING YOUR DOG

TRAINING TARGETS

The aim of every dog owner should be to have a well-behaved companion who can be taken anywhere, who fits in well with society, and who lives harmoniously with people and animals alike. While some training such as Agility, competitive Obedience or Working Trials can be considered as the icing on the cake, the bulk of your training will be a matter of teaching your dog the essentials of basic obedience, and solving problems as they arise.

If you are starting off with a puppy, your task will be much easier as you will be starting from scratch – there has been no opportunity for your puppy to learn bad habits. You can also introduce your puppy to a variety of situations, socialising him to accept the environment he is to live in. An older dog is an unknown quantity. You are unlikely to know what has happened during the dog's life to date, and therefore you will not know the underlying reason for your dog's behaviour. You will need to build up trust and confidence, and your main concern may well be solving problems rather than straightforward obedience training.

THE RIGHT APPROACH

In the past, training was normally aimed at the domination of the dog by his master. Even the use of the term "master" implies domination, both in a mental and in a physical sense. While some of the old trainers might argue to the contrary, the effect was to produce a situation where the dog obeyed because he was too frightened to do otherwise. Even women trainers developed voices like Army sergeant majors, and training sessions used to echo with bellowed commands. Experience has taught us that brute force and ignorance are not the most effective methods of training, and with some of the larger, tougher and highly-intelligent guard breeds, the method is counter-productive. Breeds like the Rottweiler have no intention of being dominated or frightened into compliance, but they are quite prepared to work with you in an atmosphere of mutual respect.

Your attitude is of vital importance, as a dog is totally vulnerable in the hands of an ill-tempered or ignorant owner. The dog can suffer from the most abject misery but he lacks any form of redress, other than biting you. If the dog reacts in this way, he will be labelled vicious and will probably be put down or discarded. Obviously, a dog who bites without cause can never be condoned, but it is worth bearing in mind that many biting incidents stem from misuse or lack of knowledge on the part of the owner.

Experienced dog handlers are confident, and do not show fear of the dog. As a result they do not expect to get bitten, and because they do not expect it, it rarely happens – even though many of them are working with difficult and powerful dogs. A dog is very conscious of fear in a human. Although the human may believe that they are concealing their fear, if it is there, the dog will be aware of it. The scent of fear will unsettle a dog: he knows that something is wrong and as a result, he may become fearful himelf.

Apart from confidence, the other necessary attribute for success is the ability to control your temper, or at least conceal that you have lost it. While you may (temporarily) believe that your dog is the most stupid, stubborn, awkward animal ever created, an explosion of incandescent rage, possibly accompanied by physical violence, will achieve nothing and only aggravate the situation. The sole result of a loss of temper will be to create either fear or resentment in the dog, and you will probably undo any good work that you have done in the past. Losing your temper with your dog for his failure to understand and comply with your wishes is not the same thing as simulated, or even genuine, annoyance for a misdemeanour. A cross or pained tone of voice is an effective means of showing your disapproval. While the dog may not understand your command to fetch your slippers or walk at heel, he will soon realise from the tone of your voice that you do not approve of being nipped in the ankle, or any other misdemeanour. It is educational to watch a bitch coping with her large litter of five-or six-week-old puppies. Her roar of rage when a puppy persists in walking over her head or tries out its teeth on her teats can be most impressive. She sounds as if she is about to murder the lot of them. In fact, she does them no physical harm whatsoever, but they quickly learn that she does not approve of this behaviour.

There are no magic formulas or secret methods which will help you train your dog. Behaviour consultants or dog psychologists may be able to give you a theoretical reason for your dog's behaviour which can help you understand the problem, but the cure will almost certainly be careful repetitive training, coupled with understanding, to instil in the dog what is required or to restore its confidence. To be successful with the training of your dog, i.e. establishing a happy relationship where the dog does what you wish and enjoys doing it, you require two things, a lot of patience and a pocketful of titbits. With a dog, bribery and kindness will get you almost anything.

SUCCESSFUL OWNERS
Talking to a large number of people who are now enjoying the company of a

well-adjusted and well-trained rescued dog, we realised that almost all these owners had certain common characteristics. Firstly, they were "laid back". They were not inclined to become excited about minor canine misdemeanours, and they were prepared to try and understand the thinking behind the dog's actions. We talked to the owner of a delightful dog, who had been thrown out by his previous owner at the age of fifteen weeks because he bit everyone's ankles. As the new owner pointed out, a puppy uses his mouth in the same way as a human baby learns to test things by gripping with its hands. The puppy is not vicious, merely inquisitive. A yell of disapproval soon tells him that biting ankles is not on.

Secondly, there is no place for the inordinately house-proud. The homes we visited were happy and comfortable, but it was not a disaster if a few dog hairs appeared on the sofa or a muddy paw-print on the hall carpet. Dogs are not perfect, and like any other relationship there must be a certain amount of give and take between you and your dog. If you love your dog, you will forgive him for many minor sins. The third common characteristic shared by successful owners is that they were kindly people with a strong sense of responsibility. Many of them worked for and helped their fellow human beings in other fields, as well as caring for dogs. When we talked to owners who had struggled with extremely difficult dogs, they all said the same thing: "I took the dog home with me so it is now my responsibility." The fact that as many as six other people had owned the dog before and had abdicated responsibility when problems arose, was no reason for the current owner to do the same.

Many of the successful owners that we met would not be considered "dog experts", in the sense that the term is often used by people involved in the world of dogs, and they would not make such a claim themselves. The world of pedigrees, breeding, showing and judging is not relevant in this instance. The secret of successful rehoming is a love of dogs, coupled with the right attitude. This means approaching the task of making a happy home for a rescued dog with patience, kindness, understanding, sympathy and commonsense – and with these ingredients, success is almost certainly ensured.

TALKING TO YOUR DOG

You should talk to your dog. This does not merely entail issuing commands when you require something from your dog – you should actually hold conversations with your canine companions. The conversations may appear to be a little one-sided, but, in fact, the dog will listen and will take guidance from the tone of your voice. Leaving aside, for the moment, the various commands you will teach to your dog, what you say to your dog is not important. However, the tone with which you say it is vital. Your dog will quickly learn that you are a person who feeds, houses and protects him. However, even before your dog learns to love you for doing these things, he will not wish to offend such a benefactor. While the words may have no meaning, your dog will be extremely sensitive to the manner in which they are said. Something said in a disappointed or cross voice will signal that you do not like what your dog is doing. The same words in a soft, possibly higher-pitched voice will indicate that you are pleased with him and the dog will respond. It follows that commands to desist will be short and sharp while requests to comply will be soft and encouraging.

An obvious example is calling your dog to you, for which you will probably use the command "Come", preceded by the dog's name. Even though you are about to be late for an appointment and are being driven to fury by the dog's tardy reaction, you will only make matters worse by using an angry tone for the command. The dog will realise that you are cross and see no benefit in coming closer to your wrath. The alternative of an encouraging soft voice will be far more effective. Do not worry about your own image with fellow humans. We can think of a number of excellent trainers, some of them large macho males, who see nothing wrong with walking around a training ring bent almost double and crooning baby-talk to encourage a new youngster to walk on the lead.

Carrying on a conversation with your dog, even when you are not requiring anything from him, brings you both closer together. You may share your opinion of the television programmes with your dog or make comments about your mother-in-law that you would not dare make to anyone else! It also serves to keep the dog's attention when you want him to keep still – when you are grooming or putting on a lead. As we said, your dog may not understand all that you are saying but he will react to your voice and your tone.

PUNISHMENT AND REWARDS

Like humans, dogs learn from the result of committing a given action. If the result is pleasant then the dog will tend to do it again. If the result is unpleasant, then he will be less likely to repeat it. Retribution or admonition for wrong-doing and reward for good behaviour must be immediate. Although a dog will remember some things for the whole of his life, punishment will not be related to misdeed unless it comes as a virtually instantaneous reaction. The experts reckon that the time-lag should be as short as half a second, or at least no longer than two seconds. If you come home to a dog lying peacefully in his basket while your best slippers are in ruins, the dog will not connect your fury to the slippers. He will merely decide that you have come home in a bad temper. Furthermore, if this happens too often the dog will start to dread your return and calm his nerves by chewing something else. You should not allow immediate admonition to turn into protracted nagging on your part. As far as the dog is concerned, he has stopped doing what you complained about and he cannot understand why you are still chuntering on. In fact, once the incident is over, you should resume normal relations with your dog with a few kind words.

Because it is essential that retribution should be an immediate result of misbehaviour, you have to solve the problem of the dog being out of your reach at the time of the offence. In general, you will have to rely on your voice. However, if you are within short range you can throw something in the direction of the dog – without hurting him – and this will bring the dog's attention back to you. The harmless guided-missile has the additional advantage that the dog does not associate it with you, but with the offence that he was committing at the time it arrived. Actual physical punishment is not really effective and will almost certainly do more harm than good. As we said at the beginning of this chapter, it will result in a dog who is either afraid of you or resentful. With a large dog, slapping him with your hand will probably be interpreted as play, and the dog may repeat the offence in order to continue the game. Praise and reward are a more important part of training than retribution. We would go as far as to say that there may be times when crimes are better unpunished, but good deeds and compliance with commands should always bring some sort of benefit either in kind or by verbal approval, preferably both. Praise should always be as effusive as you can make it and may be either given for a job well done, or as encouragement during the performance of the task. After all, the dog has just stopped doing something that he wanted to do or has complied with your wishes, so you can at least show that his cooperation is appreciated.

UNDERSTANDING COMMANDS

You may well ask, how do you actually teach your dog to understand a command. After all, he does not initially understand the meaning of the words that you are using. We have already said that a dog learns by the pleasant or unpleasant result of committing a given action. To teach specific commands you should use the command together with some indication of what is required. For example, the command "Sit" would be accompanied by a downward pressure of the hand on the dog's rump. The command and the physical indication should be repeated until the dog either complies or at least makes some move towards complying. The moment this happens, you must praise and reward the dog. Repeat the exercise a couple of times, each time praising and rewarding successful completion.

Having achieved success with an exercise, do not keep on repeating it as a demonstration to all the family of how clever you both are. Once or twice a day is quite sufficient to keep the exercise in the dog's memory. Constant repetition of the same thing will result in the dog becoming bored. It is a good idea to allocate a few minutes every day to your training rather than a major session once a week. Make up your mind as to what commands you wish to use for a given exercise and stick to them. For example, if you decide to use the command "Sit" when you require the dog to sit at your side, you will only confuse the dog if you suddenly start to say "Sit-down", especially as you will probably use "Sit" and "Down" as two separate commands requiring different actions.

NAMING YOUR DOG

The first decision that you may have to make when you take your dog home could relate to his name. Without a name which the dog recognises as his own, your training will not get very far, with the dog unable to differentiate as to whether your shouts of "Sit" are aimed at your spouse, your children or himself. You may think that as your dog had a previous owner, he would already have a name. This is not necessarily so. Some dogs have no name at all; the only command that they have ever received was a boot up the tail each morning as they were pushed out of the front door to spend the day roaming the streets. We have come across one dog who had the imaginative name of 'Dog'. There may be a connection with the fact that his owner addressed his live-in companion as 'Woman'. Other names such as 'Rambo', 'Killer' or 'Terminator' often reflect the unsuitability of the original owner.

If your dog has a name that you wish to change, then try to select one that has a similar overall sound, for example 'Rambo' might become 'Sambo'. Use the name on every possible occasion, such as feeding time, and calling your dog to you and whenever you give him a titbit. The aim is for the dog to associate the use of his name with pleasure.

BASIC TRAINING

Apart from making your rescued dog familiar with his name, the first command that we like to introduce is "No". In our household, this has the simple meaning of "whatever you are doing, stop it". "No" is a very useful word. It can be snapped out as a harsh command demanding instant obedience or drawn out in a long "Nooh" as a gentle discouragement, implying that what is being done is undesirable but not of earth-shattering importance. Use it, usually accompanied by your dog's name, whenever he does something which you do not wish him to do.

The second command which we like to bring in very early in a dog's life is another one which you rarely find in the textbooks. This is the command "Wait", which is a temporary command unlike the command "Stay", which is used to keep the dog in one spot until released. Dogs are enthusiastic joiners. Wherever you go they like to come with you, and to avoid being left behind they will give the door an enthusiastic shove at the moment that you are trying to get through it with a loaded tea-tray. In our household, "Wait" means "I am going through this door and you are not."

The same command is very useful when you are getting the dog out of the car, especially in a busy street. Because opening the car door probably means a walk, the dog's inclination is to push his way out the moment you open the door. A firm command, together with a restraining hand, will show what is required. Alternatively, you can have a helper inside the car holding the lead while you give the command.

There are a number of basic exercises which your rescued dog will need to

If you are using a check-chain as a training aid, make sure it is fitted correctly, with the chain running through the top of the loop, so that it releases automatically.

Steve Nash.

understand if you and it are to enjoy life together without conflict and even danger. Instant obedience can mean the difference between life and death, not only for your dog but for other people, if he runs out of control on a busy road. Furthermore, a dog who is aware of its place in the community is a happy dog and if your dog does what you tell him to, you will be a happy owner.

At this stage you will find it easier to teach the following exercises with the dog on a lead, although some can be practised in a few spare moments without the lead, if you are working in your fenced-in back garden. Eventually you may both be good enough for the lead to be dispensed with, but remember that your dog should always be on a lead in a public place. If you have problems, you may decide to use a choke-chain, but we suggest that you start by using your dog's normal collar and lead. All these exercises are virtually of equal importance, but we have given them in the order that is probably the most suitable.

WALKING TO HEEL

It is a vital part of your dog's training to teach him to walk alongside you, without pulling on the lead, tripping you up, or being a nuisance to anyone else. While some of this training can be done during your daily walks, you should start heelwork in the privacy of your back garden. An untrained dog will certainly pull on the lead if he thinks that he is heading for his favourite walk, whereas he knows the back garden where there are no distractions and nowhere that he particularly wants to go. Remember that your dog should enjoy his walks, which are a time for investigating new smells and sensations, and you should not spoil his pleasure by constant nagging.

The convention is that the dog walks on your left side while you hold the end of the lead across your body in your right hand. Many of us using the lead in this way allow it to run through the left hand as a means of additional control. There is no reason why you should not reverse this, except that if you eventually go to training or obedience classes you will be expected to have the dog on your left side. The aim is to have the dog walking calmly at your side without pulling ahead or having to be dragged along on the lead. The command to use is "Heel", preceded by the dog's name to attract his attention, and as you give the command you should start to walk forward. Any attempt by the dog to pull forward should be countered by a tug on the lead and a repetition of the command. If your dog drags behind, talk to him and encourage him in a gentle tone. You will find that patting your left leg with your left hand will encourage the dog to keep his head alongside your leg, and if the hand contains a biscuit or a piece of cheese, there will be even more incentive to stay in the correct position.

Frequent changes of direction will help to keep the dog moving alongside you rather than pulling away. This is one of the reasons for practising in your back garden. Sudden changes of direction on a crowded pavement could cause chaos. You should try and keep the lead slack at all times, except when it is tightened as a warning against pulling. If the lead is taut, the dog will tend to pull against it. If you tighten the lead to pull the dog back towards you, you should allow it to go slack as soon as the dog is back in the correct position.

The head collar or Halti mentioned in Chapter 3 can provide the answer to taking your dog for a walk without the outing turning into a tug-of-war, but the longterm aim should be to have a dog that is trained to walk to heel without a constant struggle. Heelwork is one of the occasions when you may find a choke-chain helpful, especially with a large dog. The tightening effect of the chain will give additional emphasis to the warning tug when the dog pulls ahead. However, do not look on the choke-chain as a means of strangling your dog to comply with your command. The same rules about keeping the lead slack apply. If you do use a choke-chain, there is a right and a wrong way of putting it on the dog. Assuming that the dog is on your left-hand side, the end of the chain attached to the lead should run over the back of the dog's neck, under the throat and back to the lead. This allows the chain to slacken as soon as you cease to pull on it. Try it on your wrist and you will see what we mean.

RECALL

In today's busy world, your dog should always be on a lead in public places, i.e. when there are other dogs, people or traffic in the the vicinity. This does not mean that your dog should be denied the chance of a gallop in an open space. A run, free of all restrictions, is one of the great joys of a dog's life, and the

*Start off by using
a long lead when
you are teaching
the recall.*

Steve Nash.

Remember to give plenty of praise when your dog responds correctly.
Steve Nash.

ideal place is in an empty park, a deserted beach, or on open moors. However, before you allow your dog to run free, you must be certain that he will come back to you when you require him to do so.

You should first practise the recall with the dog on a long lead. The extension lead (see Chapter 3) can be very useful for this exercise. Alternatively, you can carry out the training in the confines of your garden, but remember that your dog will not have the temptations and distractions that there will be away from home. Only when you are one hundred per cent certain that your dog will return on command should you venture to let him loose in an open area.

The aim is to get your dog to come back to you from wherever he is. It is an essential command for everyday life, whether you are calling your dog in from the garden or across wide open country. The usual command is the dog's name followed by "Come". Use lots of encouragement and beckoning gestures to get the dog to come to you and reward success with a titbit. If you use a word such as "Bickies" when you are normally giving him food, then try using the same word to get the dog to come to you. Curiosity works well with a dog. Waving a scarf or glove, jumping up and down, or crouching down on the ground, can make the dog come to you to find out what all the fuss is about. Your dog may be quite happily sniffing around and showing no inclination to respond to your calls, but your disappearance by hiding behind a bush or tree can make him return to where he last saw you, in case you have gone home without him.

Under no circumstances should you reprimand or punish your dog when he comes to you, even if the reason that you called was because he was doing something wrong. The experts will tell you that the recall should finish with the dog sitting obediently in front of you. So it should, but at this stage just be thankful that the dog has obeyed your command. The clever bits can come later. Some large dogs can be a bit over-exuberant on their recall, and you may be faced with an eighty-pound dog hurling himself at you. Painful as it may be, try and curb such enthusiasm gently, rather than being cross about it. If your dog is happy to come to you, you should count your blessings. Beware of the danger of your dog associating the recall with the end of a walk, and therefore being reluctant to come to you. To avoid this, recall your dog at intervals during the walk, praise, then release him again.

SIT

The Sit is precisely what the name implies: the dog takes up a sitting position on whatever spot he is standing on when the command is given. It is useful as a means of control when, for example, you are both waiting to cross the road, or you have stopped for some reason. Sitting is not a comfortable position for a dog and you should not insist on him remaining in the Sit for long periods. To teach the exercise, use the command "Sit", and at the same time press downwards on the dog's rump. Make sure that the dog is actually sitting and not merely adopting a crouched position. Some dogs will react to pressure on

Teaching your dog to sit. Use the palm of your hand in a downward motion to reinforce the command.

Wood Green Animal Shelters.

the rump by pushing back upwards. If this happens, push against the back of the hocks which will fold the dog up, rather like collapsing a folding chair.

DOWN

This command is used to get your dog lying down full-length on occasions when you wish him to remain in one location for some time. Use the command "Down" together with a downward motion of the hand and pressure behind the shoulders. You can also try rolling the dog over sideways until he understands what is required. In a dog's mind, lying down is a gesture of submission and the dog may resist until he has accepted you as the pack leader. Do not confuse the dog by using the command "Down" as an order for the dog to stop jumping up. The correct command to prevent jumping up is "No."

STAY

This exercise is used in conjunction with the Sit or the Down to instruct the dog

Teaching the Down. Use the command at the same time as making a downward movement with your hand.

Wood Green Animal Shelters.

to remain in the same position on the same spot. While your first attempts may be done on the lead, the aim is for the dog to remain in position while you move some distance away, or even out of sight. Put your dog in the Sit or Down and use the command "Stay", and at the same time hold up your hand, palm outwards. Back slowly away from the dog repeating the command. At first you should only move back a yard or so, gradually increasing the distance. This is an exercise which should not be followed by immediate praise and reward. Wait until the dog has remained in the Stay for the required time and then return, wait a moment or two and then release and reward him. Premature praise will result in the dog breaking the Stay. Increase the duration of the Stay very gradually. The dog will become bored if asked to remain in one spot for a long time.

PROBLEMS

You will amost certainly have problems of some sort during your training. In almost every case, the answer lies in being patient and in thinking the problem through. Penny, who took on Joss, a Border Collie/Newfoundland cross from Wood Green, now has a dog who is winning in both Obedience competition and Working Trials. When she got him he was rated by his previous owners as being over-boisterous and out of control. In fact, he was a large, lovable clown.

Teaching the Stay. Move slowly back from your dog, repeating the command while holding your hand palm outward.

Wood Green Animal Shelters.

It took Penny six months of patient, hard work to teach Joss to retrieve. His most infuriating trick was to take off into the far distance the moment he was released from the lead. The click of the lead clip seemed to trigger the desire to run. The answer was two leads so that his gallop to freedom when the first one was undone was brought up short by the second.

COPING WITH SEPARATION

The most popular 'buzz' phrase among canine behaviourists is 'separation anxiety'. The phrase means that your dog loves and relies on you to such an extent that he cannot bear to be parted from you. It is considered to be the cause of barking and howling, destructive chewing and fouling indoors. We would not argue with this definition. However, the solution which the behaviourists give virtually adds up to rejecting much of the affection that the dog wants to give you and reducing your own display of affection towards him. We therefore like to modify this approach as much as possible.

The aim must be to convince the dog that any separation is only temporary and that you are soon going to return. Put yourself in the dog's place. Imagine what he must feel like when the person he has come to rely on, who has taken him away from his former miserable life, suddenly disappears. The dog panics, convinced that you have gone for ever. He will sniff round the room to check where you have gone and try to follow you. Failing to follow you, he will find something carrying your scent and chew it as a relief to his nerves. You may feel that for the dog to chew one of your possessions while ignoring the toy that you bought for him, shows a lack of gratitude. In fact, he is chewing your socks or slippers because they carry your scent – and this provides some comfort in your absence.

The first obvious answer is that separation should only be for a short time. At first, leave your dog for only a few minutes, gradually increasing the time as the dog becomes more confident and realises that you will return. The total time can be longer if the dog has access to the garden or is in an outside run, rather than being shut in one room. However, in our opinion, three to four hours at a time is the longest period that your dog should be left alone. The second solution is a substitute for yourself. In other words, employ the services of a dog-sitter. This may be a member of your family or a helpful neighbour. Often a five-minute visit by someone the dog knows, at intervals of a couple of hours, will be sufficient to convince him that all is not lost.

To encourage the dog to believe that you still exist and will return, you should deliberately leave something – an old item of clothing, for example, that you have just been wearing. Just before you leave, take it off and drop it into the dog's bed or or on the floor where the dog likes to lie. Bear in mind when selecting this item that the dog may decide to chew the item into small pieces. As there are probably limits to the number of old clothes that you are prepared to write off in this way, an alternative is to keep some of the dog's chewing toys in the dirty laundry basket, handing them over just before you leave. All this may sound a little extreme, but remember that to your dog, your body odour is the most delicious perfume. Try and create an air of normality in the house by leaving a radio playing, and if it is dark or likely to become so before you return, leave a light on.

Your dog's behaviour may be affected by the way you take your leave. This is an occasion when a long and loving chat explaining that "Daddy and Mummy will only be a little time and their adorable babykins must look after the house" will have the effect of getting the dog upset and excited even before you have left. For, having aroused his interest with all the baby-talk, you walk out and leave him flat. However, if you try and sneak out quietly when the dog is not looking, he may panic when he realises that you have gone. The best option is to just give him a quiet, unemotional "Bye, see you soon" and leave, avoiding any eye contact. Apart from not arousing the dog, you will be saved from seeing the reproachful look in his eyes.

Your dog will be delighted to see you when you return. Return his affection, but try not to let him become hysterical with delight. Calm your dog with a few loving words and a cuddle, and when he has calmed down, spend some time playing with him and talking to him While your dog may be delighted at your return, the same will not apply to you if the house has been wrecked in your absence. If it has, there is no point in punishing the dog. Remember what we said about the need for punishment to be within two seconds of the offence being committed. You will never solve the problem if the dog finds that whenever you come home you are in a bad temper. Conceal your rage, clear up, and hope for more success in the future.

EXCESSIVE BARKING
A dog that barks when left alone is displaying another manifestation of separation anxiety. You may not even be aware that you have this problem until the neighbours start to complain. The neighbours may be able to help you to establish when the barking starts. If your dog starts barking immediately after you leave, then you should try and sneak back and reprimand the dog while he is actually barking. Be really cross when you catch the dog in the act. If you come back and talk to him nicely, he will decide that barking is a good idea. If you give your dog a long walk before leaving him, this will tire him and, hopefully, he will sleep rather than bark. A hungry dog is often a restless one.

HOUSE TRAINING
Failure to be clean in the house can be the result of stress from being left alone. The dog knows that it shouldn't but it just cannot help itself. The answer is to reduce the stress as we have described above.

Some rescued dogs have never been house-trained, while others may not be used to your routine. In these cases you have to train your dog as to what is the desired behaviour. Once again you must show disapproval when the dog goes in the wrong place and delight when it gets it right. Your neighbours may find it a little odd when you croon with delight as your dog squats in the middle of the lawn – but who cares if the alternative is the sitting-room carpet. Do not be tempted to show the dog the error of his ways by the old-fashioned approach of "rubbing his nose in it". This is cruel, messy and will not be understood by the dog. You should establish a routine that your dog is taken out to relieve himself first thing in the morning, at regular intervals during the day, after every meal and last thing at night.

AGGRESSION
There are two types of aggression that can apply to your rescued dog: aggression against other dogs, and aggression against humans including yourself. When dealing with both types the prime rule is to avoid confrontation. If you know that the big brute from the end of the road is likely to launch himself into an attack, then avoid going past his front gate. An unprovoked attack on a well-behaved dog can make the dog determined that he will get in first on the next occasion. Aggression against other dogs that you may meet when going for a walk should be dealt with like any other offence. Praise for good behaviour and disapproval for bad.

If you have more than one dog in your family then you may get disagreement between them. Once they are used to each other, the arguments will probably be about toys or food. You will not solve this problem by having two toys or two biscuits. The dominant dog will merely take the lot and refuse to allow the subordinate dog to share. You must allow the pack leader system to operate with two or more dogs, otherwise there will be constant squabbles. They will work out their own pecking order but you must ensure that the ultimate boss is yourself. This means that feeding and playing with toys is only done under your supervision. If you decide that you want two dogs then you will make life easier for yourself if you select a second dog who is subservient either by sex or by its nature. The junior will be quite happy to fit into the natural order of things. Some dogs, especially large males, may challenge you for the pack leadership. Training, where the dog has learnt to obey your commands will go a long way towards solving this problem. Again you should avoid confrontation and trials of strength. Wrestling with a large dog, or tug-of-war games, may appear to be fun, but when you stop, the dog will decide that he has won. When reprimanding a large dog, do not back him into a corner so that he has no way to retreat. Cornered, the dog will fight back. If your dog defies you, then the best thing you can do is to ignore him. Walk away, call the dog in a friendly manner and act as if nothing has happened. This is not the cowardly retreat that it sounds. You have avoided a battle which neither of you can win and retained the mutual respect that is an important part of your relationship.

A source of disagreement between you and your dog can arise from your wish or need to take things away from him. You may wish to rescue your shoe or pick up his food dish. You should be able to do this, but you must ask it nicely but firmly. Do not dither about. A sudden snatch to remove a treasure without warning will be resented. Use the dog's name to distract him from the object; tell him firmly that you want it and preferably offer an alternative of a biscuit or another toy.

Your dog will bark in defence of you and your household and may possibly bite anyone that it considers is attacking you. This is all that you can really expect from the average house pet and you should not encourage aggression in the dog in the hope that he will act as a guard dog. Any attempt to 'stir the dog up' and increase its natural aggression will almost certainly give you problems when his biting ability will be used on the wrong person or on the wrong occasion. The training and control of dogs for guard and attack work is a highly skilled business and should not be attempted by an unqualified person. Furthermore, if you have the dog trained by one of the many people offering this sort of service you will almost certainly finish up with a dog that you cannot handle and who will not fit into your family or the community.

TRAINING CLASSES
There are a large number of dog training classes all over the country and it is

almost certain that there is one in your area. The quality of instruction varies immensely and you should ask local dog owners whether there is one that they can recommend. Some of the instructors at these classes are of the old school which we described at the beginning of this chapter, and they will be only too keen to show you how to thump good behaviour into your rescued and possibly disturbed dog. Avoid this type like the plague and always resist the demand by the instructor to "give me the dog and I will show you how it should be done." Ask your instructor to explain what is required and then do it yourself.

A good local training class can be an opportunity for you to get help with your problems and meet fellow dog owners. A weekly training session is not a substitute for your regular daily session, but it does allow you to check on progress and pick up hints on how to proceed with the next stage of training. It also makes sure that you do at least carry out some training each week if the pressure of normal living gives you an excuse to miss some of your daily work-outs.

Training classes offer you the opportunity to progress to advanced training, such as Obedience Competition, Working Trials and Agility. Working together to achieve success in any of these competitions can be very satisfying both for you and your dog, and rescued dogs with their quick intelligence do very well. While you will make your own mind up as to which type of competition you are going in for, we would suggest that Agility is probably the best one to start with. It is fun for both dog and handler, gives both of you lots of exercise and does not have the demand for absolute perfection that is required to win in Obedience and Working Trials.

Chapter Six
HEALTH CARE

A great many books exist on the diseases and health problems that can affect the dog. Hopefully, few if any of these will affect your dog. We would suggest that excessive study of possible canine ailments can induce hypochondria in owners, leading to excessive and unnecessary vet's bills. Commonsense and good management will solve most of the problems, and much of your effort should be to aim for the prevention of illness before it occurs. Should you fail in this aim, then your veterinary surgeon has the knowledge to advise on the best treatment. In this section we will therefore set out to cover the more common illnesses and problems, their diagnosis, and the action that you should take when they occur.

Provided that your dog has come from one of the responsible breed rescue or canine welfare organisations, any major problems of health arising from his past, including those caused by ill-treatment or neglect, should have been treated and, hopefully, cured before the dog is handed over to you. If there are any residual conditions, then the welfare body should advise you what they are, and what action you need to take.

FINDING A VET
From this stage onwards, the health of your dog is your concern, aided by the expert advice of a veterinary surgeon. It would be nice to think that the only time you will need a vet is for routine inoculations, but almost certainly the time will come when you need expert advice and your dog needs treatment. Such occasions can arise at short notice, and if you need a vet in a hurry it will help if you have already established contact with a surgery, and that you have a note of the address and telephone number.

Friends and neighbours with dogs will probably be able to recommend a vet in the area that they have found satisfactory. The majority of veterinary surgeons today are in 'small animal practice', which means just what it says. The most common small animal is almost certainly the dog, although cats probably run them close. Such vets are therefore very knowledgeable about the ailments of dogs and can be extremely helpful in maintaining the health of your pet. Conversely, the treatment of dogs is probably their major source of income. It is therefore to the mutual benefit of both parties – and to the benefit of your dog – that you establish a good relationship between the three of you.

THE FIRST VISIT

Contact your chosen vet, tell him that you have acquired a rescued dog, outline the dog's past history, and give details of breed if he is a pure-bred or if he is a cross-breed, and some idea of size, age, etc.

You may have a problem with your first visit to the vet. Remember that your dog is not yet used to you, and perhaps not too confident that whatever you are doing is for his own good. The dog may not take too kindly to being taken to yet another strange place, being examined by a person in a white coat, and probably having needles stuck in his bottom. Equally, your vet will not be at all happy if his new client bites him. This first visit is a time for gentle sympathy and understanding from both you and your vet. Brute force will be counter-productive and will only give you more problems in the future. If your vet does not agree with you on this gentle approach, then you have chosen the wrong vet.

Make sure that your dog is on a properly fitted, strong collar and lead. If a dog that barely knows you breaks loose in the vet's waiting room or surgery, you are going to be most unpopular with everyone. A final word of advice on visits to the vet. We have always had a firm rule that during such visits and treatment we remain with the dog and that we hold the sharp end. We are able to talk to and calm the dog, and if anyone gets bitten it is the owner and not the vet. Incidentally, using this method we have never been bitten, and neither has our vet.

When you visit your vet with a problem, one of the first questions that he will ask is: "How long has the dog had this condition?" You may feel that he is criticising you for not taking the dog earlier. Even if you feel guilty about delaying your visit, you should give a truthful answer. It is a vital part of the diagnostic procedure for the vet to know whether the condition has existed for hours, days or weeks.

VACCINATION

Most of the major rescue organisations have a policy that all dogs coming into their kennels are automatically given standard vaccinations against certain diseases. If not, then your first contact with your veterinary surgeon will probably be when you take your newly acquired rescued dog for these essential injections. Vaccinations are given against a number of diseases, which in the past, before the introduction of protective vaccines, caused the death of many dogs. The effect of the vaccines is to produce antibodies to a specific disease, so that if the dog subsequently comes in contact with the disease, the antibodies act against the bacteria and prevent the infection taking hold. There are occasions when the vaccination does not prevent the dog catching the disease, but fortunately, with modern vaccines, these occasions are extremely rare.

The effectiveness of the vaccination deteriorates after a time, and so your dog will require booster vaccinations at regular intervals. Your vet will tell you when the booster injection is due. It is also true to say that many dogs, especially those who have been allowed to roam the streets in early life, can acquire a natural immunity to many diseases. This natural immunity can affect the effectiveness of the vaccine. If it does, then the dog probably has some immunity, but you should not rely on natural immunity to protect your dog.

The diseases which are usually vaccinated against are Distemper, Hepatitis, Leptospirosis and Parvovirosis. The vaccinations can be given from six weeks of age, but at least one vaccination must be given after twelve weeks, as the antibodies passed on by the mother can neutralise the vaccine before this date. You may or may not have been given the dog's previous record of vaccinations. If you have, show the documentation to your vet. In any case, he will give you a record of the new vaccinations, which you should keep for future reference. Furthermore, if your dog has to go into boarding kennels, you will almost certainly be asked to produce a current record of vaccinations – a policy which is important for the health both of your dog and of the other inmates.

Your vet may suggest other vaccinations. One of these is against the condition known as Kennel Cough. This can be caused by a number of different organisms, and the vaccination may not work against all of them. However, many boarding kennels do insist on this vaccination. Take your vet's advice.

DIARRHOEA

The two most common causes of diarrhoea are diet and stress, and either or both these elements may occur when you first acquire your dog. The most frequent cause of diarrhoea is a digestive problem and the bowel looseness will probably cease when the food that caused the problem is withdrawn. For treatment you should withhold all food for twelve to twenty-four hours so that the dog's intestines can settle down. During this time you must ensure that water is always available. Diarrhoea has the effect of dehydrating the dog, and withholding water will not solve the problem. If you consider that the condition is likely to be stress-induced, then in addition to withholding food you should try and create the calmest possible atmosphere. When you commence feeding again, give only small quantities and use bland foods such as boiled rice, minced chicken, fish or scrambled eggs until the dog's motions are normal.

Diarrhoea can, of course, be indicative of serious illness and if it persists after twenty-four hours of treatment or, if it is extremely severe, or if the motions show signs of containing any blood greater than a small fleck, then your vet should be consulted at once.

WOUNDS AND CUTS

A dog will lick and clean minor cuts and grazes, and this should be allowed, but not to excess. If the dog persists in licking and nibbling at the wound then you may need to use a preventative collar. Vets can supply these, but you can make a perfectly adequate one out of a suitably sized plastic bucket. Cut the bottom out of the bucket and make several holes around the edge of the narrow end. Place it over the dog's head with the wide end towards the nose and tie it to the dog's collar with string using the holes you made around the edge. Most dogs settle down quite happily wearing this contraption. They can see what is happening, eat, drink and breath, but they cannot get at the sore spot. All the same, do not make your dog wear it for too long. If you feel that the wound needs cleaning, then use a dilute solution of Dettol or TCP.

Wounds that require a bandage are best dealt with by an expert, as it is very difficult to stop the bandage slipping without making it so tight that it restricts the circulation. Bandages on legs and feet can be protected by using an old sock, which can be protected against wet by a polythene bag when the dog goes outside. Deep or large wounds may require to be stitched by your vet.

GIVING MEDICATION
Your vet will happily give you a box of pills with the instruction that the dog should have one three times a day. You will have the problem of persuading the dog to take his medicine. Putting the pill in the dog's food will probably mean that the dog will wolf his dinner and when he has finished, the pill, however small it may be, will be the only thing left in the dish. Worse still, the dog may spit the pill out and lose it so that you do not know whether it has been swallowed or not. Dogs can be extremely clever with their mouths so as to discard anything that they do not want. One answer is to bury the pill in a small but favourite titbit. The dog is so keen for the treat that he has swallowed the pill without knowing it. If this does not work, open the dog's mouth with your left hand by pushing your thumb and index finger from outside the lips in behind the upper canine teeth. Use your right hand to push the lower jaw downwards. To keep the mouth open, press the dog's lips over the molars. Push the tablet as far back as possible over the tongue. Close the mouth and hold it closed while at the same time stroking the dog's throat to make him swallow.

You cannot expect your dog to lick unpleasant-tasting liquid medicines from a spoon. The easiest way to give liquid medicines is to use a plastic syringe without its needle, which you can get from your vet. The procedure is to suck up the correct dose into the syringe and pull the dog's cheek outwards to form a pocket. Tip the dog's head back and gently squirt the dose into the 'pocket'. Lightly massage the dog's throat to encourage him to swallow. If you do not have a syringe, use a teaspoon to get the medicine into the pocket of the cheek.

PARASITES
FLEAS
Your rescued dog may have fleas when it comes to live with you. Even if it has

not, then you may still be worried that it will introduce them to your household. Fleas are difficult to find unless there are a lot of them. Use a fine comb along the back and around the base of the tail. The droppings are black in colour and the size of grains of sand. If you shake these on to a piece of damp white blotting paper and they leave a reddish stain, then your dog has fleas. If there is no stain then they are probably just grains of dirt.

Fleas are not necessarily a sign that your dog is dirty or neglected. Dogs who are well looked after can collect the odd one. In fact, to a flea, the modern house with its deep carpets and central heating is its idea of heaven. Grooming your dog regularly with a fine comb will help, and your vet will advise you on the wide range of insecticides available. You should also make regular use of your vacuum cleaner around your dog's bed, the edges of carpets, and chairs. Preferably, you should burn the contents of the dust bag. If you treat your dog for fleas, make sure you wash your dog's bedding at the same time.

TICKS

These are unpleasant, but they are not really harmful in small numbers. They are brownish-white insects, about the size of a pea, which are firmly attached to the dog's skin. The dog can pick them up from grass where they have been deposited by sheep or hedgehogs. They will drop off when they have had their fill of blood, but you do not really want to have them dropping off around the house. If you pull them off you may leave the head embedded in the skin, which can cause an infection. The best method is to use tweezers and dab the spot with disinfectant, or use a piece of cotton wool soaked in surgical spirit to make the tick loosen its grip.

LICE

These can only exist on the host animal, so that there is not the problem of infestation of carpets, furniture etc. The adult lice are brown insects which move slowly on the skin. The eggs are white in colour and can be seen attached to the dog's hairs, usually around the ears and neck. Use an insecticide to get rid of them.

MANGE

The two main forms of mange are sarcoptic, which can be passed on to humans, and dermodectic which does not affect them. Frequent and violent scratching and patchy loss of hair may indicate mange. Consult your vet if you think that your dog has this condition.

ROUNDWORMS

Young puppies almost invariably have roundworms, and even healthy adults may carry a mild infestation. The technical name for this parasite is Toxocara canis. The worms are round, white in colour, and about three to six inches in length. They are passed by the dog either singly or in a bundle of two or three, and may be passed with or without faeces. Much has been made by the anti-dog lobby of the fact that the eggs of these worms can affect humans. For this to happen, the egg needs to be swallowed, and even then it is very rare for the human to suffer any ill effects. However, there have been a very small number of cases where more serious harm has been done. Obviously you do not want to put other humans, especially children, at risk, even though the risk is extremely small.

The eggs need some time to mature after being deposited, and it is therefore commonsense to pick up and dispose of all faeces as quickly as possible. The adult dog produces less eggs than a puppy, but you should make a practice of worming your dog at least once every six months. Some of the worming treatments available from pet shops are not completely effective, but your vet will be able to supply effective modern treatment and will advise on the correct dosage for your dog. Many of the modern wormers destroy the worms within the dog so that they are not visible when passed, thus relieving you of the unpleasant task of shovelling them up. However, although you cannot see any worms, this does not mean that you can stop your regular worming. The combination of regular worming and good standards of hygiene will mean that any risk to yourself or your children will be reduced to infinitesimal odds.

TAPEWORMS
This is a segmented tapeworm with a small head, which attaches itself to the wall of the dog's intestine. The segments break off and appear in the faeces. The flea plays a part in the life cycle of the tapeworm, so that your anti-flea campaign will help to reduce the chances of your dog having a tapeworm. Once again, the person to see is your vet, who will provide a remedy. If your dog needs such treatment, your vet will need to know the weight of your dog.

DERMATITIS
Some dogs have very sensitive skins and a small irritation such as a flea bite or scratch will cause them to lick or bite at the area. The damaged area is then infected by bacteria, causing further inflammation and irritation, which can spread rapidly if not treated. The area will be inflamed and ulcerated, and bare of hair. You can ask your vet to treat this condition, but we have found that it is simple to treat at home.

Clean the area thoroughly, using a diluted solution of antiseptic such as Dettol or Savlon, and make sure that you remove all pus. Then dry the area gently and apply an ointment such as Germoline, which is both antiseptic and a local anaesthetic. The local anaesthetic helps to stop the dog aggravating the condition by further nibbling and scratching. In most cases, this treatment will quickly control the condition. The area will dry up and you then have to be patient while the hair grows again.

The above list of creepy-crawlies and horrible beasties may appear to be rather off-putting, but keeping any animal can involve such troubles. The important thing is to be able to recognise the condition before it becomes a major problem. While you need to be aware that such things can occur and be able to diagnose them, in actual fact you will, hopefully, have very little cause to worry about the occurrence of most of these ailments. Good management, correct feeding, regular grooming, and commonsense will keep your dog a fit, healthy, and happy member of your family. It is also important to maintain strict hygiene, e.g. washing hands, whenever you have to treat your dog, and this limits any risk of diseases being transmitted from animal to man.

INHERITED CONDITIONS
ENTROPION
This is a hereditary condition found in some dogs, usually those which have a background of certain breeds where the condition is fairly common. It shows itself as a wet patch below the eye; often the eye is partially closed and the eyelid is swollen. The dog may rub its eye with its paw. The condition is caused by the eyelid turning inwards so that the eyelash irritates the eyeball. Owners of dogs showing such symptoms will often claim that the dog has been sitting in the car with its head out of the window. Maybe it has, but if the condition persists you should consult your vet, as it can be extremely painful and can result in permanent damage to the eye. The condition is easily cured by a simple surgical operation.

HIP DYSPLASIA
You may hear this phrase, often abbreviated to HD, mentioned as being of major importance in the world of dogs, together with the need to identify the condition by means of X-rays. Dogs with severe HD should never be used for breeding, and this is why identifying the condition is so important. However, if you have no plans to breed from your rescued dog (and in many cases your dog may well be neutered already), you can forget all the about the problems of HD, unless your dog becomes extremely lame for no obvious reason.

HD is a hereditary condition in which the hip joint becomes malformed. Many dogs have it to a degree, varying from very slight to severe. The vast majority lead perfectly normal lives with no reduction in their agility. There is no cure other than a fairly major operation. In order to X-ray your dog for HD, a general anaesthetic is required which is both costly and puts your dog at risk, and so there is no point in doing it merely to establish that your dog has the condition.

EMERGENCIES
MAKESHIFT MUZZLE
Muzzles can be bought from pet shops, but there may be times when you need

to improvise a muzzle – if you need to do something with your dog which he resents, or if he is injured. You will need a length of bandage or you can use a nylon stocking or half a pair of tights. Work from behind the dog and place the middle of the bandage on top of the dog's nose in front of the eyes. Pass the bandage under the nose making a simple knot under the jaw, then take the bandage back behind the ears and tie again. It is a good idea to practise this in a quiet moment. This is an effective method of muzzling which does not restrict the dog's breathing, although your dog will look at you with a soulful expression while wearing it!

ROAD TRAFFIC INJURIES
All dogs should be kept under strict control in areas where there is traffic, but accidents do happen and you may find yourself called on to help a stray dog who is the victim of a road accident.

Your first problem will be to stop the traffic. Other drivers may not see that there is an injured dog in the road, while others will merely drive round it and resent any delay. A dog that is in shock and pain will possibly bite instinctively, so, if possible, wear thick gloves. Throwing a coat over the dog's head will help to restrain it and protect you. The dog may have injuries which will be aggravated by being moved. However, if the dog is in the road you will have to move it, and you will probably have to get it into a car so as to take it to a vet. If possible, move the dog gently on to a blanket or sack and slide it along. Any bleeding wound should be covered with a pad and gently bandaged or held in place. Drive as steadily as possible to the nearest veterinary surgeon, keeping the dog warm with some sort of cover while you do so.

Veterinary surgeons will rarely come to the scene of an accident, and the police will be reluctant to attend if a dog is the only casualty. Some animal welfare organisations have animal ambulances on call, but these are rare. In most cases, there is no apparent owner of the dog and no identification on the collar. Once you have got yourself involved, you are likely to find that everybody else is content to leave things to you, including the payment of the vet's bill. The only compensation is the hope that if it was your dog, someone else would be equally kind and caring. Thankfully for both dogs and the community, not everybody "passes by on the other side."

OLD AGE
Among the dog-lovers we most admire are those who make a practice of giving a comfortable, loving home to old dogs who have only a year or so to live. Usually these are dogs whose owners have died, leaving them alone. Giving a home to such a dog can be both heartbreaking and expensive. When you take on a young dog, you have a reasonable chance that you have ten or more years together; with an old dog the end comes round all too soon. However, those that take on the 'oldies' have the reward of knowing they have provided a

home and companionship at the evening of a dog's life. Inevitably, the young dog that you rehome will grow old and your routine together may have to be adjusted. Illnesses such as kidney or heart disease may require special diets; your vet will give advice on this. As the amount of exercise the dog takes is reduced, the amount of food required becomes less. However, it is not always easy to harden your heart when food is one of the few pleasures left in life, and your dog's appetite remains as before. While you are not doing your dog any favours by allowing him to become overweight, a slight middle-aged spread brought on by a few extra morsels of his favourite food will do no harm.

The old dog may become hard of hearing. The fact that your dog no longer responds immediately to your commands may be the result of deafness rather than stubborn old age. Eyesight can also deteriorate, and the happy smile of greeting can lose its bright-eyed gleam. Age brings a desire to sit closer to the fire, and an old dog needs a warm and comfortable bed out of the draught where he can sleep undisturbed. The length of the daily walk may have to be reduced, while at the same time the dog's bladder may not be as strong as it used to be, so that he requires to spend a penny more frequently. Exercise may therefore become a matter of shorter, but more frequent walks.

As you see your dog grow older, you may feel that you would like to have another younger dog before the old one dies. Think carefully about this. If the old dog has been the only dog in the household for many years, he may not take kindly to having part of your affection transferred to an 'interloper'. If a dog has given you his trust for most of his lifetime, perhaps he deserves your undivided attention in old age. In any case, a boisterous youngster may be too much for the old dog's patience. This could lead to arguments which the older dog may not win. Equally, some old dogs, especially males, can take on a new lease of life with a puppy, and will behave like a proud grandparent.

DEATH
Regrettably, dogs do not live as long as we do. If you are lucky your old dog will quietly drop off to sleep in his basket and not wake up. A dog who dies in this way, without pain or distress, saves you from making the decision that comes to almost all dog owners – and for many of us it comes far too often. While old age in itself can never be a good reason for putting a dog to sleep, there can come a time when incurable illness and physical deterioration can reduce the dog's quality of life to an unacceptable level. For many people the idea of putting an old and trusted friend to sleep is a decision that they cannot face. But no matter how painful, we believe this decision must be made. After a long and happy life together the final duty that you have to your dog is to give him a peaceful and painless end. If you allow your dog to linger on in pain and with loss of dignity, then you are being kind to yourself while being cruel to the dog.

A veterinary surgeon can put a dog to sleep without distress or discomfort to the dog. The dog does not know what is going to happen, and provided that you are with your dog holding and talking to him, then he will slip peacefully away. However distressful it may be for you, you must stay with the dog until the end. To allow your dog to be dragged away by a stranger into a strange place, probably to be injected after a struggle is the final betrayal of all that you and your dog have meant to each other.

You have one more unhappy task. Many people like to give their pet a grave in a quiet corner of the garden. Visitors to large country houses will have seen under the trees in the park a group of tombstones bearing names like 'Spot' or 'Blackie', often covering a hundred years of the family's pet dogs. Modern small gardens do not lend themselves to this arrangement and a grave under the apple tree may not be practical, especially for a large dog. The alternative is cremation. There are a number of organisations offering cremation, either en masse, which probably does not appeal to you, or as an individual cremation of single dogs with the ashes being returned to you for scattering in your garden or on some open space where the dog loved to play.

While the death of your dog can be a cause of distress for yourself, your own death will leave your dog in need of help. You may leave behind someone who loved your dog as much as you did and who will continue to care for him. If so, then you have no need to worry; but with nothing being certain in life except death, you would be wise to make some legal and firm arrangements for your dog's care. Many of the major animal charities operate schemes whereby they will carry out your wishes in the event of your death.

It is important that you allow the charity some flexibility in how they carry this out. Instructions that are too rigid may commit your dog to spending the rest of his life in kennels. While the dog will be well looked after, this may deny him the chance to build a new life in another family. On the other hand, you may be worried that the rescue organisation may rehome your dog in an unsatisfactory home, and the dog would be better off leading a safe but dull life in the kennels. There is no easy answer, and you must assess the quality of the organisation and make up your own mind. If you have friends or relations who are willing and able to take on the responsibility of caring, then you might consider making provision in your will for some form of trust fund to cover the costs of looking after your dog for the remainder of his life.

The death of a much-loved dog is certain to leave a large gap in your life. Some of us wish to mourn quietly for a time before looking for a replacement, others are anxious to replace the loss as soon as possible. Perhaps the best memorial that you can give your pet is that you give a fresh life and happiness to another dog who needs it. When you do replace your old friend, remember that the new dog will be a different individual, with different characteristics. Love your new dog for what he is, and do not expect him to be an exact duplicate of your old companion.

Chapter Seven
DOGS AND THE LAW

In the past, dog ownership was a very innocent thing. The family dog, a man walking his dog, and children playing with a dog were part of everyday life, almost part of folklore. Dog ownership was simple. If you wanted a dog then you had one. There was a thing called a dog licence, but it only cost 7 shillings and 6 pence (37 1/2p), and increasingly fewer people, including the Government, bothered with it as it was too expensive to enforce. The law concerning dogs was largely covered by legislation going back over a hundred years which said, in simple terms, if your dog attacked humans or other animals or made a nuisance of itself in various ways, then you could be taken to court. The action taken by the courts was largely at the discretion of the magistrates and could vary from a small fine, an order to keep the dog under control, or in serious cases an order for the destruction of the dog. The attitude was one of commonsense, coupled with a general feeling that the dog was a well-liked member of the community.

THE CHANGING SCENE
To a certain extent, the change in attitude towards dogs by both Government and the general public can be blamed on dog owners themselves. The large increase in the number of people keeping dogs, especially in urban areas, coupled with the attitude of many owners that "the dog can do no wrong", led to a variety of problems. These included excessive fouling by dogs in the streets and in public places, incidents of biting, and the use of dogs as a defence against the police by criminal elements. The "latch-key" dog, turned out on the street first thing in the morning and left to roam the streets, often in packs during the day, became commonplace. Ordinary, decent dog owners were slow to realise what was happening, and, while they could not stop the criminal misuse of dogs, for a long time they failed to take action on such aspects as fouling and keeping their dog under control.

The small but vociferous anti-dog element seized on these aspects, and in the late eighties they began a campaign for far tougher laws on dogs in general. A number of tragic incidents, which involved dogs in attacks on children, highlighted the whole problem of irresponsible dog ownership. Fuelled by pressure from the media, the Government decided it must act swiftly to introduce legislation. The very fact that this was done in haste means that, while some elements are quite reasonable, other parts are difficult to implement and do not necessarily get to the root of the problem. However, it is important that all dog owners know the requirements of the law.

DOG WARDENS
Local authorities are now required (under the Environment Protection Act) to appoint an officer responsible for dogs, usually known as an animal or dog warden, to carry out the various requirements applicable to dogs in their area. Such wardens may be council employees or may be working on an arranged contract. The best of these contracts are with animal welfare organisations, so that the wardens have the support and expertise of the organisation behind them. The knowledge, attitude and efficiency of dog wardens varies immensely, as do the standards demanded by local authorities. In general, wardens are either dog lovers with at least some vocation for the task, or they are merely dog-catchers. If you meet your local warden at obedience training classes, judging local dog shows and lecturing to school children, then you probably have a warden who will interpret their job as largely educational; they will carry out their work with sympathy and understanding.

A major part of the dog warden's job is the collection of stray dogs. There is no statutory definition of a stray dog. However, the law considers that it is reasonable to assume that if a dog is running loose in a public place with no person apparently in charge of it, then the dog is a stray. This is where the problems can start. There are many dogs who know exactly where they live, but are in the habit of taking a stroll round the block each morning. They like to check on the availability of any bitches in the area, make sure that there are no rival dogs encroaching on their territory, and probably pick up a biscuit from the kind lady on the corner. Under the old legislation the police had the discretion to decide whether the dog was a stray or not. The local bobby would recognise Fido, and knowing that he lived at No.9 and had never caused any trouble, would allow the dog to go on his way.

The present law *requires* the warden to seize any dog that he believes to be a stray. Provided that the owner of the dog can be identified by the name and address on the collar, the warden is required to notify the owner of the fact that the dog has been seized, of where the dog may be recovered, and of the fact that the dog may be disposed of within seven days if it is not claimed. The law lays down that recovery will cost the owner the sum of £25, the cost of any kenneling, plus any other reasonable costs such as the dog warden's time. It is now a legal requirement that all dogs should wear a collar bearing the name and address of the owner/keeper. You may be taken to court and fined if your dog is found not complying. It is obviously essential that you do not allow your dog to roam unaccompanied outside your own property.

DOG-FOULING

Dog fouling is dealt with under local authority byelaws. The local authority is required to keep its roads and other lands free of waste, which includes dog droppings. They are therefore empowered to introduce byelaws which either ban dogs from certain areas, or require the owner to clear up after their dog. The penalties for offending in this way are becoming more and more severe – with fines as high as £200 or more. Responsible dog owners should therefore go equipped when walking their dogs in a public place. All pet shops sell 'pooper-scoopers'; plastic bags are equally suitable, and bins are usually provided for disposal of waste.

LEAD CONTROL

Strictly speaking, you are not required to have your dog on a lead at all times when on the public road. However, the Road Traffic Act 1988 authorises highway authorities to designate certain roads where a dog must be kept on a lead. Such roads must bear signposts so that dog owners are aware of the order. Commonsense must tell you that it is sensible to keep your dog on a lead – no matter how perfectly he may walk to heel – in any area where there is traffic or where your dog can cause annoyance to other people.

BARKING

Noise from a persistently barking dog can land you in trouble – it can constitute a statutory nuisance. The fact that you had no problems until your new neighbour started complaining will not always be a successful defence.

THE DANGEROUS DOGS ACT

The most disturbing dog legislation is contained in the Dangerous Dogs Act 1991. At the time of writing, attempts are being made to have some aspects of this Act amended, but it is unlikely that those parts which are likely to affect you and your rescued dog will be changed to any major degree. The Act actually deals with two different but linked issues. The first part deals with action against certain breeds or types; the second deals with dangerous dogs in general.

The first part of the Act introduces special controls for four "types' of dogs. They are:

1. The Pit Bull Terrier.
2. The Japanese Tosa.
3. The Dogo Argentino.
4. The Fila Braziliero

If, on reading the last three names on this list, you say that you have never heard of these dogs, you may be forgiven. Although we have been involved in

THE RESCUERS

ABOVE: Aerial view of the Margaret Young Home for Animals, Wood Green Animal Shelters, Godmanchester.

Wood Green Animal Shelters.

BELOW: Sadie, happy, friendly and clever, is now enjoying a full and exciting life with her new owner, Joy. She was found wandering the streets and was taken to Wood Green Animal Shelters for rehoming.

Cambridge Newspapers Limited.

ABOVE: Some rescued dogs need special love and care to help them get over the trauma of their former life. Tessa, anxious about being left alone, would pile everything that was moveable in the kitchen and sitting-room in one large heap, and would then go to sleep on top of it. Wood Green Animal Shelters.

RIGHT: Samantha, the Beagle, eventually overcame her anxiety problems, and her owners were encouraged to take on Boots and Maxwell, two more dogs in need of rehoming. Wood Green Animal Shelters.

Muttey, the ugly duckling who turned into a swan. According to his owners, Muttey looked so odd when they first saw him, no one seemed to want him. The benefits of a caring home are clear to see.

Wood Green Animal Shelters.

STAR PETS

Author Jilly Cooper is a great Champion for the cause of rescued dogs. Hero and Barbara are her devoted companions.

Favour, the first Hearing Dog for the Deaf, chosen in 1982 from the National Canine Defence League.

Albert Rigby APRS

Hearing Dog Sally Ann, adopted from the RSPCA at eighteen months of age, now working in Derbyshire.

Hearing Dogs for the Deaf.

LEFT: Shep was found after he was thrown out of a car on the motorway. Now trained as a Dog for the Disabled, Shep has transformed the life of his owner, Ann Greenwood.

Dogs for the Disabled.

BELOW: Helping with the shopping is one of the many tasks that Shep has been trained for.

Dogs for the Disabled.

The best of friends, Louis and Storm. Louis, a German Shepherd/Tervueren cross was rescued by the RSPCA. After months of loving care, Louis settled down in his new home and has won over thirty awards in Obedience competitons.

Benson: The greatest reward of rehoming a rescued dog is the love and trust your dog will give you.

Wood Green Animal Shelters.

The Dangerous Dogs Act,
introduced with the
intention of eliminating the
American Pit Bull Terrier
and other fighting breeds
from Britain, has resulted in
many problems resulting
from mistaken identity.
Buster, a cross-breed, was
saved from destruction only
after his owners had fought
a costly court battle.

dogs for over forty years, we have yet to meet a British dog expert who has seen either a Dogo Argentino or a Fila Braziliero – the two South American breeds – in the UK. As for the Japanese Tosa, one male was imported just prior to the Act being drafted. The most extravagant claims were made in the media as to its size and ferocity, and before the solitary Tosa had time to settle in, it found itself banned.

The real cause of the problem was the Pit Bull Terrier. This dog has been bred in the USA for many years, produced for the sole purpose of dog fighting. The British Kennel Club has refused to recognise the Pit Bull as a breed. To be fair to the Pit Bull, almost any dog will fight under certain circumstances, and the Pit Bull's crime is that in it, man has developed a dog which is a more efficient fighter than most other breeds. Apart from its fighting ability, the Pit Bull is just another dog, with all the good and bad characteristics of any dog. However, in addition to its use for dog fighting, the Pit Bull Terrier has also been used as a guard dog for criminals – especially those involved in drug trafficking. The Government decided that there was no place for this dog in Britain and passed the Dangerous Dogs Act with the intention of eliminating it. It has declared that it is illegal to own or import any one of the four dogs listed, unless a certificate of exemption has been obtained. To obtain a certificate of exemption, the dog must be neutered, permanently implanted with an identifying transponder, tattooed with an identifying number, covered by third party insurance, and recorded on the Index of Exempted Dogs. The dog must be kept in secure conditions at home so that it cannot escape. In a public place it must be muzzled and held on a lead by someone who is at least sixteen years of age. The penalties for infringement of the Act include a fine and/or imprisonment.

The aim of this legislation is to eradicate the Pit Bull and other alleged fighting dogs. However, there is a flaw in the drafting of the legislation which can bring heartbreak to perfectly innocent dog owners, who have no intention of getting involved with dog fighting or any other illegal activity. Those who drafted the Act realised that it would be virtually impossible to prove in a court of law that a dog was of a particular breed. To avoid this problem they added the word "type" to the description. The Pit Bull Terrier is a fairly nondescript animal, and it is easy to find mongrels and cross-breeds which approximate to its description, especially when it is interpreted by people with little or no knowledge of dogs. To complicate the legal tangle still further, the Act reverses the burden of proof, making the owner prove that his dog is not of the Pit Bull Terrier type, rather than the age-old right under the law of a person being innocent until proved guilty. This requirement, coupled with the fact that it is a crime to own a dog of this "type" which has not been registered under the Act, means that an innocent owner whose dog happens to fit the description, could find himself in court struggling to avoid punishment and the destruction of his dog. Both the courts and the animal welfare bodies are becoming aware of the possibilities for injustice contained in this Act, and if you and your dog are unfortunate enough to face prosecution, there is now a considerable amount of expert assistance available. Since you cannot alter the appearance of your dog, your best chance of avoiding any problem is to ensure that he is well trained, under control, and that he does not behave in a way that could be construed as being the behaviour of a Pit Bull Terrier.

The second part of the Dangerous Dogs Act deals with dogs of any breed which are dangerously out of control in a public place, or in a private place where they are not permitted to be. The Act defines "dangerously out of control" as any occasion on which there are grounds for reasonable apprehension that a dog will injure any person, whether or not he actually does so. What constitutes "reasonable apprehension" is, of course, a matter of opinion. A large dog jumping up or barking in greeting may be construed by someone who knows dogs as harmless high spirits. To a person afraid of dogs, it can appear to be threatening to life and limb.

If the court decides that a dog is dangerously out of control, the owner or person in charge of it can be imprisoned and/or fined. Should the dog be so out of control as to injure someone, then the courts are obliged to order its destruction. Section 3, which covers this requirement, applies to any breed of dog, be it a Yorkshire Terrier or a Great Dane. As before, the answer lies with commonsense, training and consideration for the rights and feelings of other people. You have a duty to your dog and to the community to ensure that neither the one nor the other suffers as a result of your negligence.

BYELAWS

A certain number of rules that can affect your dog are local byelaws and other regulations. These obviously vary from district to district. Some housing authorities and some private landlords place restrictions regarding their tenants on the ownership of dogs. Some of these are discriminatory with regard to the type of dog that you keep. A typical example is a blanket ban on dogs, except by special permission. This allows the landlord to permit or turn a blind eye to the ownership of some dogs, while banning others. Inevitably, these decisions can come down to a matter of personal prejudice against certain breeds.

SUMMARY

It is regrettable that in a book devoted to the pleasures of owning a dog there is a need to get involved in the possibility of legal problems. There is no doubt that some of the restrictions which we now suffer have been the fault of irresponsible dog owners in the past. It is therefore essential that all dog owners are aware of their responsibilities and do not contribute to a demand for further restrictions.

Chapter Eight
SUCCESS STORIES

Rescued dogs have repaid their rescuers by going on to serve mankind in many ways. Dogs from rescue kennels are working for the deaf and for the disabled, as therapy dogs for the sick and as search dogs for the police and armed forces. Others have confounded those who threw them out as unwanted by becoming stars in Working Trials and Obedience. The vast majority have been successful by becoming much-loved members of families.

STAR PETS
Many rescued dogs have become the beloved companions of people who are famous for their achievements in all walks of life. This is an example of charitable work by the wealthy and successful that is not solved by merely throwing money at the problem or making a token appearance. Such owners go through the same problems arising from ill-used and unwanted dogs as the rest of us. There is a very long list of well-known personalities who have given homes to rescued dogs or who in some cases have done the rescue work themselves. The famous author and journalist Jilly Cooper describes herself as a "mongrel addict". Because the terms 'rescued dog' and 'mongrel' tend to become synonymous, many of the numerous dogs in her life have been rescued dogs.

Jilly's book, *Intelligent and Loyal* (published by Eyre Methuen, 1981), sings the praises of the mongrel dog, with hundreds of anecdotes ranging from the horrific to the hilarious. When you talk to Jilly you realise her enormous love and enthusiasm for the entire canine race. Asked about her preference for mongrels she makes it clear that she is by no means anti the pure-bred dog, but she feels that the mongrel needs all the support that it can get.

Her first rescued dog was acquired as an antidote to an impossible English Setter. He was rescued from a gang of louts who were about to stage an execution by hanging. His new home, after being saved, was not a success, and he was taken on by Jilly. Her husband named him Fortnum. Fortnum must be one of the few mongrels who has some offspring born "on the right side of the blanket", in that his fatherhood is acknowledged and approved of by his owner. Reading Jilly's description of his skill and enthusiasm as a stud made us wonder whether he might have played some small part in formulating some of the human characters in her novels! Two of his puppies from two separate litters, Mabel and Barbara, have joined the Cooper household.

Jilly has taken a long look at the retained memories of rescued dogs, working out how something that happened in the unhappy days before they came to their present home can affect their behaviour. Fortnum was probably running loose in the streets as a tiny puppy on Guy Fawkes night and was always pathologically afraid of thunder and fireworks. He was a real canine street-corner boy. Living at the time in Putney he quickly established his territory, locating all the interesting dustbins and likely females. From the very beginning he knew his way home, barking to be let in when he became too fat for the cat-flap. Sadly, Fortnum has gone. Most of us have had one extra special dog in our lives. For Jilly, Fortnum was that dog.

Today she has one of his daughters, Barbara, now growing a little grey around the muzzle, and another rescued bitch, Hero. Hero is a lurcher and the sole survivor of what appears to have been a canine massacre. Her mother and three sisters were found drowned and it is not known how Hero survived. She was rescued by the National Canine Defence League Kennels, from where she came to Jilly. She has never lost a certain fear of the world, but in spite of being of a type bred to pursue small animals, she gets on well with the household cats and kittens. One of her habits, probably caused by nerves, is that she likes to chew the toes off shoes – although not when they are being worn. She does a quiet tour of the guest bedrooms when they are empty, and more than one overnight guest has left the next morning looking a little odd around the feet.

BALLY'S STORY
Television personality Lloyd Grossman tells the story of his rescued dog, Bally:

"The family – wife Debs, three-year-old Florence, and three-month-old Constance – were on holiday in Ireland. Driving along the road to Schull, where our favourite pub is, we were heading down the hill into the village of Ballydehob when we saw a small caramel-coloured dog wandering along the roadside, a common enough sight in West Cork. 'Doesn't she have a sweet face?' one of us observed. Two or three hours later, on our way back through Ballydehob, we saw the same dog again near the same spot. Only this time she was wandering along the road, inexpertly dodging traffic.

"We stopped the car, put on the emergency flashers and tried to get a closer look at her. With rather ill grace she let us look her over: no collar, very smelly, rather lame, tumour on her back, milky eyes. We couldn't leave her to be run down. So we loaded her into the car – much to the bemusement of our dear Westie, Betty – and drove off to the local police. They couldn't keep her, they said, but would keep their ears open for reports of missing mutts. We took her back to our house and bathed her gingerly, taking the completely unnecessary

Television personality Loyd Grossman pictured with his rescued dog, Bally, and Betty, the family's West Highland White Terrier.

Colin Poole.

precaution of tying a bandage around her muzzle. She accepted her bath like a stoic, ate a couple of tins of sardines like a wolf, and was altogether gentle as a lamb.

"We made regular trips to the local vet in Skibbereen, who, freshly returned from delivering a calf or nursing a horse, began to patch up our mutt. Thankfully, no one ever came to claim her, and ideas about rehousing her with a local family remained ideas. She came back to live in London with us. When people ask us what she is, we say that she's a West Cork terrier; she certainly has a family resemblance to hundreds of tinkers' and farmers' terriers that you see in the West of Ireland. She has ridiculously long ears, a huge bottom, big feet, skinny legs, a leathery belly and an indescribable coat. She is slightly daft, unfailingly polite, stubborn as any other terrier, and devoted to the children. We call her Bally – short for Ballydehob, the village where our love affair with her began."

SEARCH DOGS

Our first experience of dogs used to search for specific substances was in Malaya in the 1950s. Dogs used for police work, tracking and man work were normally members of the large guarding breeds. However, one of the problems of the anti-guerrilla campaign was to find hidden caches of food, usually rice. To search for these we used fat and rather greedy little mongrels who would snuffle around in the jungle until they suddenly sat down wagging their tails.

Digging on the spot would reveal a bag of rice.

Today dogs are used to search for both drugs and explosives. Most of these dogs are gundogs or gundog crosses, and many of them come from rescue kennels – an example of the dog not merely helping mankind but actually saving human life, sometimes at the expense of their own.

DOGS FOR THE DISABLED

Working on the same principle as Guide Dogs for the Blind, this organisation trains dogs to help the disabled carry out everyday tasks which they cannot cope with unaided. Generally, the organisation uses dogs that have been rescued, giving the double advantage of enabling the dog to serve mankind while being given a loving home at the same time. Much of the success of this scheme stems from the mutual reliance, respect and understanding between two beings, both of whom have suffered pain and adversity. Dogs for the Disabled also uses dogs specially bred by Guide Dogs for the Blind who have failed to show the special qualities required for guiding work, but who are able to work successfully for the disabled.

The files of Dogs for the Disabled are full of case histories of rescued dogs providing the equivalent of a vital pair of hands or feet for their handicapped owners. Tasks which are simple for the rest of us, such as opening a door or picking up a dropped pencil can be impossible or very difficult for the disabled. Dogs are giving them independence and a new life. It takes about a year to train a dog and their training is tailored to the individual needs of each owner. Many

Dog for the Disabled Poppy, with owner Amanda.

Dogs for the Disabled.

of the dogs used are of Border Collie type, fairly light in body and gentle in nature.

Gina suffers from spinal muscular atrophy and has been in a wheelchair since the age of four. When she was twenty the doctors said that she had only ten to fifteen years to live. Then Ben, a gentle German Shepherd, arrived. Gina now rejects the forecast of her life expectancy. As she puts it: "There is no way that I am going to die before Ben, I wouldn't trust anyone else to look after him."

Ann Greenwood has spent her life with horses. Before she became confined to a wheelchair she ran a riding stables. Disablement meant that she could no longer ride, and even driving a pony and trap was impossible without the help of friends. Shep, a Border Collie trained by Dogs for the Disabled, changed all this. Shep was thrown out of a car on the M6. He had chased every blue car that came along in the vain hope that it belonged to his owner. When he was finally caught he had worn away his pads until he was unable to walk on them. For three weeks he had to be carried everywhere, even to spend a penny. The memory of this terrible trauma has stayed with him. Some three years later when Ann drove Shep up the M5 to take part in a television programme, they approached a busy stretch of motorway similar to where he had been found. Shep, normally a good traveller, started to cry and was violently sick. Something had triggered his subconscious and revived memories of the trauma that he had been through.

Shep is a very bright dog. When he was handed over to Ann he understood some forty commands. He would answer the phone, by picking it up and bringing it to Ann, he could turn lights on and off and pick things up and retrieve. His repertoire has now extended to over one hundred different words and tasks. A television team once expressed surprise at his ability. Ann said: "Alright, I will teach him to identify one of you by name." It took half an hour, after which Shep would pick up an object and take it to the named person. Given a problem he will try and work out the solution for himself. One of his tasks is to open and close the stableyard gate. Normally he just pulls on a rope hanging from it. One day a high wind made this impossible. After several attempts Shep found the answer. He jumped and hung on the gate so that the weight of his body pulled it closed. He shows no fear of horses and is always available to fetch grooming brushes and feed bowls. He will happily walk underneath the pony and bring harness straps from one side to the other so that Ann can fasten them. He was a bit baffled by a tiny Shetland pony who was too low to the ground for Shep to walk under but he worked out that it was possible to crawl under with the strap.

Another of his regular tasks is a visit to the mobile shop which stops at the end of the drive. He sets off carrying a basket containing the order and money, and returns with the groceries and change. Ann teaches music at the local school, and Shep barks when they arrive so that the access ramps can be put in place. He is a great favourite with the children, and one little girl who had been badly frightened by a dog has regained her confidence through the gentle attentions of Shep. He is always at Ann's side and is so busy that she has found it necessary to feed him an extra high protein diet. He is on call twenty-four hours a day but this does not stop him occasionally relaxing and playing with the other dogs. Like many good-natured dogs he is also a tease and will play games with Ann, while never forgetting his responsibilities and duties.

"Shep has changed existence into living for me," said Ann. "He has given me independence, freedom, and above all, companionship. If he did not do all the things that he does, he would still be my best friend."

HEARING DOGS FOR THE DEAF

Dogs working for Guide Dogs for the Blind and Dogs for the Disabled use physical skills to perform tasks which are impossible or extremely difficult for their owners. Hearing Dogs for the Deaf are trained to draw their owners' attention to specific sounds which need their attention. For a deaf person it is obviously useless to use the dog's normal method of attracting attention by barking. Instead, they are trained to identify a number of different sounds, alert their owner by a touch of a paw, and then lead them to the sound source. Typical sounds that they are taught to identify are an alarm clock, the telephone, the doorbell, a baby alarm and a cooker-timer. One exception to the standard reaction is if a smoke or fire alarm goes off, when the dog is taught to alert the owner and then drop to the floor to indicate the potential danger.

The idea of a dog using its hearing to replace that of a human started in the USA with the Hearing Ear Dog program. The first dog to be trained in Britain was selected from the National Canine Defence League kennels by Pat Riley, the American trainer, in 1982. The dog selected was a rather skinny white cross-breed, with large warm brown eyes. As with so many dogs taken from rescue kennels, he appeared to be asking to be chosen. He had been found wandering by the side of the M4 motorway and was about one year old. He was sponsored by the American insurance company, Mutual of New York, and he was given the name Favour.

For some ten years Favour worked as a fundraiser and demonstrator. He became a seasoned television performer and featured in numerous newspaper and magazine articles. Although he was a great success in his new career, Favour remained a bit of a lad and liked to relax with the sort of adventure which street dogs have always enjoyed. As a result he collected the odd scar and battle honour. He retired after ten years service, a bit stiff in the joints and beginning to slow down. He will always be the dog who became the pathfinder for yet another service by dogs for humans.

Hearing Dog Sally Ann, sponsored by the Salvation Army, was adopted from the RSPCA at about eighteen months of age. She had already served her apprenticeship as a rescued dog, having been in three homes including Battersea, but was still a happy, alert, intelligent character. She is now the constant companion of Sara Head, a profoundly deaf young woman, who is a teacher at Derby's Royal School for the Deaf. Sally Ann attends all Sara's classes and gets her own good behaviour symbol – a bone – on the class reward chart.

Looking at a large number of case histories of rescued dogs working both with the disabled and the deaf, we find there is one constant factor. In every case, apart from carrying out the tasks they have been trained for, the dogs also give companionship, loyalty and love to their owners. The therapeutic help given by these dogs is virtually as important as their trained function.

LOTTIE'S STORY

Looking at the success achieved by a rescued dog and his owner, it is important to bear in mind the situation and condition of the dog before his rehabilitation began. The more dreadful the dog's previous life, the greater the achievement when he rises above it. The story of Lottie is worthy of inclusion in any canine hall of fame.

Lottie is a Rottweiler bitch. She was frequently picked up in the streets of South London by the police or the RSPCA and returned to her owners, who were known as drug addicts and generally undesirable. Lottie and another bitch had been bred from, a number of times, as a money-making proposition. Rescue workers in some breeds have to be physically tough as well as being kind-hearted and gentle. When Lottie's frequent visits to the police kennels became known, it was arranged that when her next visit had exceeded the statutory seven days, she would be moved to the welfare kennels. It would not be the first time that rescue workers had found it necessary to 'persuade' an owner that their dog would be better off in other hands. Lottie duly arrived at Rottweiler Welfare. Her condition can best be described by Pauline, the welfare worker who first took her in:

"I cannot adequately express my feelings when I first saw Lottie. One ear was completely torn off, with the scar extending across her head and down across the corner of her eye. Half the other ear was missing and there was a large bare flesh wound on her left flank. Her legs were covered with burns, probably made with lighted cigarettes. It is almost certain that she had been used as "bait" for dog fighting while muzzled."

After this sort of treatment, Lottie could be forgiven if she hated all mankind. Far from it, as Pauline relates: "She was so loving and gentle and trusting. I just wanted to hold her and love her and tell her that no one would ever hurt her again."

Lottie settled down very quickly. She made friends with the other Rottweilers, and she was a bit spoilt – although she deserved it – as she was allowed to sleep indoors and had quite a lot of extra cuddles. Well-wishers donated funds for her upkeep and for her to be spayed. The vets found her a model patient and were very impressed. While recovering from her operation,

Lottie, the Rottweiler, still bears the scars of her former life. She is now the mascot for Rottweiler Welfare and is their chief fundraiser.

Rottweiler Welfare.

she and Pauline slept in the lounge together, as Pauline did not want her to fret.

From the beginning Lottie showed no signs of aggression, but she was afraid of men, which was hardly surprising in the circumstances. We first met her when she made her debut at a large dog show some few months after she was taken into care. No one could have called her beautiful with her torn ears and body scars still showing red and raw. However, in spite of the physical damage her mental attitude seemed unharmed. Many of those who saw her had a lump in their throat and tears in their eyes, but she charmed everyone with her gentle loving nature. She also charmed the general public into filling her Rottweiler Welfare collecting box, and the trade stand holders donated lots of their products.

After her first outing it was decided that she should become the mascot to Rottweiler Welfare. As Pauline was very much involved in fostering other welfare Rottweilers, she felt that she could not give Lottie all the attention that she deserved. Lottie moved in with Lynn, and she now enjoys all the delights of living in the country with five other dogs. Lottie now works very hard to repay those who have helped her. She has qualified as a PAT (Pets as Therapy) dog, and makes regular visits to a residential home for the elderly, where she is thoroughly spoilt and much-loved. She also makes regular trips as a charity collecting dog, collecting for human as well as animal charities, not forgetting her old people's home. She has passed the stringent breed character assessment gaining the grade of "Excellent", and has been awarded the Bounce Super Dog medal for her courage, devotion and charity work, plus many other awards. She is much in demand for public appearances, including the Crufts Personality Parade, and has made numerous appearances on television.

Lottie must be considered a superb example of a dog rising above her misuse by man. Apart from her general success, she has done much to change the unfairly adverse image of her breed which was created by the campaign against Rottweilers.

FAMILY FAVOURITES

The greatest success story concerning rescued dogs is, on the face of it, the least spectacular – it is the thousands of ordinary dogs in ordinary homes. For these owners, the success lies in overcoming all the difficulties, heartbreaks and expense that can be involved in rehoming a rescued dog. These are the real success stories. Visiting a large number of homes with rescued dogs, we found that the owners had become totally committed to this type of dog. Some were on their fourth generation of dogs from rescue kennels. Others were so pleased with the first dog they homed, that they went out and added another one or even two more.

In one home we only expected to see Samantha, a rescued Beagle. She had been with her present owner for six years and was on her third settee having demolished the first two. To be fair, she wrecked these during her first year, and is now such a reformed character that she prefers to be known as the 'Duchess'. Her eventual good example encouraged her owners to acquire a pocket-sized Beagle, named 'Boots'. This name is an abbreviation of "these boots were made for walking". He was taken by the shelter kennel to a sponsored dog walk as a spare dog for anyone willing to join in who did not have a dog. Nobody needed him, and his present owner, taking pity on the little wallflower, walked him home for good. Boots became number two.

Number three, Maxwell, a Harrier rather than a Beagle, had a lucky escape. Released to run loose in a raid upon an establishment breeding dogs for research, he was caught and taken to the rescue shelter. His spell of running wild meant that he was no longer clinically sterile, and therefore of no use for research. Maxwell joined Samantha and Boots.

Samantha started badly. She was obviously insecure and although little was known of her previous history, she had been thrown out on the grounds that her owners could not cope with her. She tried to alleviate her frustration by chewing and destroying the furniture. If she had been human, she would have chewed her fingernails or taken up smoking. It took a year and a number of trips to the secondhand furniture shop, but gradually she began to realise that her home represented love and security, and that there was no longer the need to soothe her nerves by chewing.

Boots has given very little trouble. Being small he can get to the places that other dogs cannot reach. One of these is the mantelpiece over the sitting room fireplace. Reaching this point of vantage via the arm of the chair, he will perch there looking like a rather lifelike Staffordshire model. He also likes to yodel. His rather high-pitched howl is echoed by Samantha, with Maxwell singing bass.

Maxwell had been bred and reared in a kennel with virtually no contact with the outside world. He was almost a wild dog, frightened by everyday sounds such as a radio or a washing-machine. He knew nothing of humans, other than the few who had fed him and cleaned his kennel. He showed no aggression to people; they aroused neither fear nor affection, merely indifference. This was a dog that had been produced as a neutral, sterile, standardised piece of living tissue for the sole purpose of research. His house training was non-existent. While he would not soil his actual bed, anywhere else, including the middle of the sitting room carpet was alright as far as he was concerned.

Slowly he gained confidence in his new owners. The solution to his lack of house-training was an indoor cage fitted with a bed which took up the total floor space of the cage. He would sleep quite happily in this, but it was obviously essential that he was taken outside as soon as he woke up. In his mind, the cage became sanctuary to him. So much so that, being a smart dog, he quickly learnt to use his paw to undo the bolt and open the cage door when he wanted to retreat to safety in it. It took eighteen months and a lot of patience to persuade Maxwell that it was a good idea to be clean in the house, and that he had both a home and a future. He also did his share of destruction around the house including £20 worth of books, belonging to a friend, that had to be replaced.

As a group the three dogs are happy together. Being hunting dogs they are prone to deciding that they are a pack if a rabbit appears when they are out for a walk. Their owners have given a lot in time, money and understanding. In return, they have three dogs who are now well-behaved and who love them and are loved in return.

Tessa lives in a small house in a country village. It is a 'lived in' home, comfortable and full of things connected with the family's interests. Their previous dog, who had been thrown out of an American air base at the age of nine months, had lived to the ripe old age of seventeen. Looking for a replacement, the family went to Heydon Animal Shelter. Walking around the compound full of dogs of all sizes and shapes, one particular dog decided she had found the family she wanted. She followed them everywhere and seemed determined to be chosen. Eventually they asked the shelter to keep her for them until the weekend.

Tessa's record from her previous owner was horrendous. She was uncontrollable, threw herself against walls and had fits – hardly the sort of recommendation that would make her attractive. Many of those who take on a rescued dog are of the opinion that few dogs are really hopeless, and they also welcome a challenge. Tessa was lucky or perhaps clever – she had found such an owner. For a few days, all went well. Tessa seemed to have found her niche. Then the time came when the family had to go out and she was left alone for a few hours. They returned to find a worried neighbour waiting on the doorstep. "I don't know what has been going on, but there has been a terrible noise from your house," she said.

In the sitting-room they found Tessa. She was sitting on a mound comprising everything movable from both the sitting-room and the kitchen. The curtains had been pulled down and piled with the cushions. Books, potted plants and ornaments were added to the heap. The only access that Tessa could have had to the kitchen was through a service hatch which was about four feet from the floor. Through this hatch she had brought kettles, saucepans and anything else that was portable. She must have worked very hard for quite a while, and it is not surprising that the neighbours commented on the noise. In spite of the massive removal operation, nothing was torn or broken.

A wire-pen was built in the garden. Three times Tessa demolished the gate, and when this was made unchewable she ripped up the wire fence instead. It was obvious that having found her family, the big worry in Tessa's life was that she would lose them again. The fear that they would not come back was more than her nerves could stand. For a year Tessa was never left alone. Luckily, other members of the family whom she loved, lived in the village. They took it in turn to babysit with her. Towards the end of this period, her owners took her with them on a caravan holiday. Spending all her time with them, she was well-behaved. However, as they got close to home she started to cry and became restless. She bounded up the drive, in through the front door and settled into her basket with a positive sigh of relief. Home again! Holidays are alright, but its good to be home. From then on, Tessa has been a model dog. At last she believed that she was safe and secure for life.

Tessa's owners are keen on DIY, and she likes to help. To her, ladders are things a dog can climb, and she has discovered that you can see far more of what is going on from the top of one. She likes to join in, and she is quite capable of opening doors so that she can join the party. She insists on being the centre of attraction and will even climb on to the table if she feels that she is being neglected. She loves the grandchildren, and she is happy to wear three leads at once so that they can all take her for a walk. Some things still upset her – she still howls when the telephone rings – but as her owner says: "A rescued dog always has its past lurking in the back of its mind."

HONOURS IN OBEDIENCE

Most rescued dogs are of medium size, but Louis, a German Shepherd /Tervueren cross, and Storm, a Bernese Mountain Dog, come within the category of large dogs. Louis was one of thirty dogs removed from a kennel by the RSPCA. He was eighteen months of age and covered in mange. He had never been inside a house and was totally unsocialised. He was, and to a certain extent still is, claustrophobic. He spent much of his time in his new home sitting at the bottom of the garden howling. Although he now sleeps in his owner's bedroom, all the doors, including the back door into the garden, are always open and at intervals through the night he will trot downstairs and into the garden to make sure that his escape route is still there. At first he showed his insecurity by burying things in the garden. Not just the odd bone but major items like large tins of meat and the contents of the laundry basket. On one occasion his owner was puzzled at the loss of several of her children's T-shirts, until she noticed a tiny scrap of material sticking out of one of the flowerbeds. Investigation produced the missing shirts.

It took some six months for Louis to settle down. When you visit him you meet a large, gentle dog who sits quietly at the side of his owner. He shows no objection to your presence, but ignores you or moves away if you make any attempt to pat him. Periodically he will check that the back door is still open. He submitted to being 'bossed' by the fourteen-year-old cat and allowed the twenty-year-old cat to use him as a bed. Louis has won over thirty awards in Obedience competitions and at Exemption Shows. He is a very handsome and impressive dog, who always catches the judge's eye as being the sort of dog that one would like to take home.

Strictly speaking Storm does not qualify as a rescued dog as he was bought from his breeder after being rejected by three different homes as being uncontrollable. After six months of patience and love he has settled in as part of the family and shows no signs of being the tearaway that he was reputed to be. The two large males live together without friction and one senses that they each rely on the other for support in coping with the world. Their owners have worked for many years in the care of mentally handicapped children, and perhaps the qualities which enable them to solve the problems of such human teenagers are the same as are required for dealing with traumatised dogs.

OUTSTANDING BOOKS ON YOUR BREED FROM
RINGPRESS

Britain's leading publisher of quality books for pet owners

The award-winning BOOK OF THE BREED series offers unrivalled expertise on individual breeds. The books average 60,000 words and more than 100 photographs, all written by internationally-known experts. Current titles in the series include:

AKITA

AUSTRALIAN CATTLE DOG

BASENJI

BERNESE MOUNTAIN DOG

BEARDED COLLIE

BORDER COLLIE

BOUVIER DES FLANDRES

BOXER

CHINESE CRESTED

GOLDEN RETRIEVER

GREAT DANE

GERMAN SHEPHERD

GERMAN SHORTHAIRED POINTER

GERMAN WIREHAIRED POINTER

GORDON SETTER

GREYHOUND*

HUNGARIAN VIZSLA

ITALIAN GREYHOUND

LABRADOR RETRIEVER

MASTIFF

OLD ENGLISH SHEEPDOG

PAPILLON

RHODESIAN RIDGEBACK

ROTTWEILER

ROUGH & SMOOTH COLLIE

SALUKI

SHIH TZU

SHETLAND SHEEPDOG

ST BERNARD

STAFFORDSHIRE BULL TERRIER

WEIMARANER

WEST HIGHLAND WHITE TERRIER

WHIPPET

YORKSHIRE TERRIER

All priced £15.99 *(Complete Book Of Greyhounds £17.50)*

The PET OWNER'S GUIDE series offer EXPERT ADVICE and STUNNING COLOUR PHOTOGRAPHY at a budget price. The books average 25,000 words and 60 colour photographs for just £4.99. Current titles in the series include:

GERMAN SHEPHERD

LABRADOR RETRIEVER

GOLDEN RETRIEVER

SHIH TZU

POODLE

YORKSHIRE TERRIER

SHETLAND SHEEPDOG

ROTTWEILER

DALMATIAN

Ringpress titles are available from good bookshops everywhere.
In case of difficulty order direct from:
Ringpress Books Ltd., P.O. Box 8, Lydney, Glos. GL15 6YD
For a free copy of our catalogue send sae to the above address.

At Wood Green, caring is just the beginning ....

ANIMAL CRISIS

This is Buster. He is one of the lucky ones.

We receive thousands of animals whose families have had to give them up because their domestic circumstances have changed (Buster's owner had to go into a home but many are from house repossession) or because of personal tragedy.

Nearly all our cats and dogs, including Buster, are rehomed and go on to live happy and fulfilled lives. To help prevent further problems, we offer pet counselling, training and home visits to ensure that all our animals have the best possible chance.

We even offer to record your wishes for their future should anything happen to you - free! (Pet Alert Scheme) and of course we also run the National Pet Register.

All this costs money and to continue this valuable work, we would be grateful for a donation of any size or just to be able to send details on the Shelter and our various schemes. For more information or to send a donation, please contact us at :

Heydon,
Near Royston,
Hertfordshire SG8 8PN.

Tel : 0763 838329
Fax : 0763 838318

WOOD GREEN ANIMAL SHELTERS

REGISTERED CHARITY 298348. A COMPANY LIMITED BY GUARANTEE (NO. 2073930)